no thanks OR REGRETS

Edited and introduced by

Jacqueline Kent

STATE LIBRARY OF NEW SOUTH WALES
PRESS

No thanks or regrets
State Library of New South Wales Press, 1996 ©
Macquarie Street, Sydney, NSW 2000 Australia
(02) 230 1514

© text, individual authors
Anthology edited and introduced by Jacqueline Kent
Cover design by Tania Edwards
Text layout and design by Wellington Lane Press Pty Ltd
Reproduction photography by Image Library Photographic Service
Printed by Southwood Press

ISBN 0 7310 6604 9

National Library of Australia Cataloguing-in-Publication data
1.Short stories, Australian. 2.Women authors, Australian –
Biography. 3.Australian fiction – Women authors. 4.Biographical
fiction, Australian. 5.Autobiographical fiction, Australian.
6.Australian fiction – 20th century. I.Kent, Jacqueline, 1947–.

A823.0108492

CONTENTS

INTRODUCTION

Jacqueline Kent

No thanks or regrets, this was my chance for adventure writes
Jane Seifert in her story 'About Time', giving this anthology its title and its theme. For this collection of stories
deals primarily with women's adventures; not the take-
me-to-Timbuktu kind of adventure, nor the science-fiction
sort we know from movies and TV shows. These adventures range from the horrors of a Nazi concentration camp
to discovery of a new sexuality, from carving out a new life
in the opal wilderness of Australia to the life of a thirteenth-century nun.

The stories were written for a competition held by the
Society of Women Writers NSW Inc. to celebrate its seven-
tieth anniversary. Each, submitted under a pseudonym in
the first instance, had to be 'an autobiography or biography ... based on the experiences of a woman in Australian
life'. Judges Margaret Jones, Barbara Jefferis and Judith
Kelly all noted the diversity of styles and subject matter.

'Replay', which gained first place, sets the theme in an
interesting and highly imaginative way. Pippa Kay uses
a computer game — perhaps the ultimate 1990s adventure? — to take us through the stages of a woman's life.
The metaphor is very effective: like life, the game does
not allow the player to skip over any painful sections,
and the player is allowed to speculate about what might
have been.

The dramas in Pippa Kay's story are mainly domestic: not so two stories with the self-deprecating 'Life' in the title. Anneliese Stricker's story, simply called 'A Life', is the story of an unnamed German woman who suffered under Hitler's Reich and fled to Australia just before World War II broke out, only to find that life here had its own difficulties. 'My Two Lives' by Lottie Weiss tells of surviving life in the concentration camps. Both these stories gain power from their prosaic narrative styles; there is no need to underscore the horror of the events they describe.

Thanks and regrets are featured, however, in Mary Devenish's 'Events in the life of a sixteen-year-old alcoholic'. The subject and narrator, a young Aboriginal girl, tells what could easily be a depressing story: how good, then, to find that this one has a happy ending. And, true to the same spirit of survival, at the end of 'About Time' Jane Seifert proposes a toast to life, to Australia, to the future.

'If history is a checklist of heroic deeds produced by men ... how can women's achievements be recognised?' asks Susan Steggall in 'Taking the Tally', her fascinating parallel study of St Clare of Assisi in the thirteenth century and Sister Angela of Australia's St Clare monastery in the twentieth. As the author points out, both were women who lived creative lives in a 'man's country', where the land itself often dominates and is dominated by the masculine, and both had to reinterpret that world for themselves.

A male-dominated world is also the milieu of 'Opal Fever' by Karen Heap, a breezy and conversational account of going bush to become an opal miner. Its emphasis on a life where practical skills define success and identity makes an intriguing contrast with some very 'female' stories. Both Rae Luckie's 'The Prolapse' and Robyn McWilliam's 'A Touch of Trauma' (about having breast cancer) graphically describe the extent to which we are defined by our physical identities, how circumscribed by the bodies we were born with.

But Katherine Cummings, in 'Life and Loves of an XY Woman' also shows that femininity can be chosen. She describes her struggle to become the woman she has always been in spirit, despite being born into a male body; the price is to be 'left in a limbo of loving'. If, as she says, her emblem is a butterfly, it is one with sharp teeth and claws and the will to use them.

It remains to consider a group of stories that come under the heading of traditional biography; the life stories of apparently ordinary women. Rae Luckie's 'Kit' and 'Memory' show that scraps of everyday writing saved from a woman's life — lists, letters, diaries — can be laconic records of both hardship and heroism. Ba Phillips' 'Small-Eye', the story of a woman's last days in hospital, becomes even more poignant when one knows that the author herself has since died of cancer. And it reinforces the theme of 'Sister' by Gabrielle Bates, which is about confronting fear by turning it into art, enabling us to endure the unendurable.

In a paper written for the pre-competition seminar, novelist and critic Barbara Jefferis wrote: 'Biography and autobiography seem to me just as creative as fiction. The difference lies in the difficulties. Writing fiction is simple, compared with writing biography. Fiction has no shape, no texture, no flavour until the writer gives it one. Real life, either past or present, has a shape of its own ... for me the real key to good biography is this — looking into your character is only half the battle. The other half — maybe the better half — is looking out from your character, seeing the world through his or her eyes.'

Without regrets, the contributors to this anthology have made us see the world through their eyes, and we thank them for it.

Sydney, 1996

REPLAY: AN AUTOBIOGRAPHY

Pippa Kay

'I've got a new computer game,' said nineteen-year-old son, between mouthfuls. 'It's hard. You have to set goals and when you achieve them you get points.'

'How many lives do you get?' asked twenty-one-year-old son who, having finished his dinner, pushed his plate away.

'Only one.'

'That stinks! What's for dessert, Mum?'

'You'll find some ice cream in the freezer,' I told him. While he fixed plates of ice cream for himself, his father and brother, I sipped my wine and contemplated the problem of having only one life. In computer games you usually get three or more.

While they were eating dessert their father mentioned the need for study. The boys nodded their heads like puppets. I tried to tell them, 'It's not like a computer game. You don't get unlimited chances in real life.'

'But that's where you're wrong, Mum,' insisted nineteen-year-old son. 'With this new game, if you make a mistake then you have to go back to the beginning and start all over again.'

'How do you win?' asked twenty-one-year-old son.

'I don't know yet. I had just started playing when Mum called us for dinner.'

'What sort of weapons do you have?' asked the twenty-one-year-old son.

'You don't really have weapons. You don't have anything much to start with, just yourself and a long road you have to go along. You can't see the end.'

'Then how do you know when you've finished?'

'I don't know, I'll tell you when I get there.'

After dinner nineteen-year-old son disappeared into the study to the computer. He soon became frustrated with the game and was yelling at the monitor. His father threatened to turn the machine off if he didn't keep the noise down. After loading the dishwasher I had a look at this new game. On the screen I could see what looked like a tunnel.

'It's not a tunnel,' he said. 'It's a rut, and I can't get out of it.'

'Well, how did you get in there?' asked twenty-one-year-old son.

'You don't want to know.' He rolled his eyes, looking and sounding more and more like his father.

'Well, if you go back and retrace your steps surely you can get out,' suggested his brother. 'Here, let me have a go.' He pushed the backspace button, the computer beeped and the screen said:

*** ERROR ***
Press ESC to exit or SPACE to continue

Then the tunnel-like landscape reappeared on the screen.

'See what I mean,' said nineteen-year-old son. 'If I press escape then I'll have to start all over again. I've done that once already.'

'It's only a game,' his father reminded him. 'Surely you've got some study to do.'

'I want to have a go,' said twenty-one-year-old son. 'How do I start?'

'Press ESCape, then at the C:> type in LIFE.'

'Is that what it's called? Life?' I asked.

'Yes, it's a stupid game. I wish I'd never started.' He stormed out and slammed the door.

I had trouble sleeping. Living in a house with three grown men can be difficult. My sons were adamant that they knew more about the computer than their father and the evening had ended with tempers flaring, doors slamming and my husband accusing me of not supporting him. The computer game was the problem. My understanding of computers is limited; I only use ours for word processing. The boys seemed to believe that having only one life was unreasonable. My husband was convinced that there was a virus in the machine and was blaming the boys for indiscriminate use of shared software. I couldn't believe a computer game could cause so much trouble.

Restless, I left the bedroom, went into the study and turned on the computer.

C:> LIFE

It was like looking into a mirror. My own reflection on the computer monitor. Was I dreaming? I pressed F1 for HELP.

C:> F1/Help

> ### Do you want to play the game of life?
> ### Y (Yes) N (No) ESC (Exit)

C:> Yes

A road that ran off the screen.

> ### SPACE to continue, ESC to exit

C:> SPACE

The cursor moved slowly along the road. I saw myself a tiny dot on the screen.

C:> F1/Help

> ### Alt Z for Zoom.
> ### Magnification level:
> ### 1 = 100%; 2 = 200%; 3 = 300%?

C:> Alt Z, 3

I'm wearing my red dress with white dots and I'm in the lane outside our home in Tasmania. There are blackberries growing on the fence opposite and I'm covered in blackberry juice. Daddy is coming with a big stick. I'm running away. He catches me at the end of that road, where there is a beach. I run toward the water. Mummy screams my name. A wave breaks over my head. Daddy pulls me out of the water.

That was close. Too close. I change the magnification level: Alt Z, 2.

... living in Padstow in the 1950s. The Queen is coming. Nanna takes me to see her, but all I see is legs, ladies' dresses and men's trousers. I can't see Nanna's and I am crying.

'Did you see the Queen?' asks my mother.

'No I didn't,' I tell her, wiping the tears from my eyes.

C:> Pause

Pause/Break

Hold on, I tell the computer, while I get some tissues.

C:> Alt Z, 2

The road takes me to my first school. I'm tall for my age and they think I'm older than five. My teacher discovers I've got spots all over me. Mummy comes to school and takes me home. I've got chicken pox.

C:> Pause

Pause/Break

There must be a short cut. I've got measles, mumps and tonsils to go yet. How do I get to the good parts?

C:> F1/Help

Ctrl S = Control Speed
1 = slow, 5 = medium, 9 = fast

If I speed it up I can skip the childhood illnesses.

C:> Ctrl S, 9

Infants' school, copybook writing, times tables, playlunch, warm milk, peanut butter sandwiches, detention, homework ...

So fast I feel dizzy. Slow it down a little.

C:> Ctrl S, 5

New school: Methodist Ladies' College. Hat and gloves. Assembly and prayers. 'Walk as daughters of the light.' Christmas holidays, living at Gladesville. Watching 'Six o'clock Rock'. My eleventh birthday and my best friend Sandra goes to another school.

C:> Ctrl S, 1
Looking for tortoises in the bush behind Gladesville Psychiatric Hospital with Sandra. I've started having periods but Sandra has not.

Two young men meet us and say they know where there are tortoises. We follow them away from the creek up a hill into a gum forest. They want me to kiss them but I don't want to. One holds me while the other removes my skirt and panties. Sandra sits on a log and cries. I'm pushed to the ground. I'm going to be raped.

C:> Pause
Pause/Break
Do I really want to be reminded of this? I try a faster speed.
C:> Ctrl S, 9
*** ERROR ***
Press ESC for exit or SPACE to continue
C:> SPACE
One is lying on top of me, and he's trying to push his penis into my vagina. I shut my eyes. I can hear Sandra crying. The other one slaps her and tells her to shut up. Then he says it's his turn. The one on top of me tells him 'Bugger off.' He has his pants down, his penis is huge and he's trying to put it in my mouth. I could bite it off, but I scream instead. I'm choking.

'What's going on up there?' A man's voice from down near the creek. They pull up their trousers and run away.

Sandra says we shouldn't tell but I think we should. I try to explain to Sandra but she doesn't know the facts of life yet. Sandra drags me away. I feel sore and sticky between my legs. We go to her place where no one else is home. In the bathroom I see that I am bleeding. I'm frightened because it's not time for my period.

I go home by myself. I'm late and shaking so much I can hardly talk. They call the police and I'm asked questions. 'How far did he penetrate? How many inches?' I don't know. A doctor examines me and I scream again. I'm given an injection that makes me sleepy. I don't tell anyone about the man putting his penis in my mouth.

My father searches the road and the bush with the police. They decide it's best to pretend it never happened. They think they were patients from the hospital. I'm told never to talk about this to anyone and never to see Sandra again.

C:> Ctrl S, 9

I let the early years of high school spin past while I get a small whisky from the bar in the lounge room. When I return to the screen I've met Jim, my first boyfriend. I slow the game down because this may be interesting.

C:> Ctrl S, 1

Kissing and petting on his bed in his flat. The song on the radio is 'Young girl', and I'm his young girl. He's a schoolteacher and I'm a student. I want to leave school and marry him.

He tells me that I've got to study for my exams and he'll not see me for a few weeks.

After the exams, he doesn't ring me. I wait and wait by the phone. When I write a letter to him it is returned unopened. He doesn't live there any more. My mother suggests he may have another girlfriend, someone more his own age. I don't believe her.

C:> Ctrl S, 9

I make myself another small whisky, thinking that I'd better go easy on the alcohol.

I watch the screen flicker through the rest of high school and the early years of university. It takes until the end of my first year of Arts to recover from Jim.

I see him while I'm driving. He's about to cross a road at a pedestrian crossing, near where he used to live. He sees me through the windscreen and I note the surprise in his eyes, but then he looks the other way. Too cowardly to say 'Hello'.

C:> Pause

Pause/Break

What if I did marry him? Could I, through this game, see what would have happened?

C:> F1/Help

C:> WHAT IF?

I expect to receive the ERROR message but I watch the road on the screen split and I find myself on a branch road. I put my whisky down on the desk and, with both hands on the keyboard, tap the space bar lightly.

There's a woman I don't recognise. It could be me, but I don't think so. Her hair is greyer, her face is lined and she looks much older than I do. Her eyes are sad. I walk through her house and look out the windows. There are brick walls blocking them. I open the back door and am confronted with another brick wall.

Like my son's rut, I think. Now what do I do?

C:> BACKSPACE　　　***** ERROR *****

Press ESC for exit or SPACE to continue

I stab at the keys.

C:> SPACE, F1/Help, Ctrl S, 9

I want to get out. What if my husband comes in and finds me playing this computer game? How would I explain this?

I see Jim. He's ageing before my eyes like film in fast motion. I ask him the way home but he doesn't seem to see or hear me. I don't belong here. Then the woman comes to him and they hold hands. I follow them out the door. They turn to the right and follow the branch road to wherever it may go. I don't want to know. I see Jim drop a letter in a letterbox, marked Return to Sender. I'm free to continue on my own way again. The branch road disappears.

C:> Ctrl S, 5

I sip my whisky while I watch the university years roll by. There are parties with rough red wine in flagons and spaghetti bol. I smoke a little marijuana, a friend attempts suicide after taking LSD.

I meet the man I'll marry and decide to take these scenes slowly.

C:> Ctrl S, 1

He has a beard and long hair. We are both studying for exams. There are essays, exams, good friends and high romance — well, mostly. One night he says, 'You know, I think we ought to get married,' and I accuse him of having too much rough red.

He's finished his studies and I'm nearing the end of mine when we decided to tell my parents. He doesn't ask my father, he says: 'I think I might like to marry your daughter'. And my father, who had been hoping for something more definite, says, 'And pigs might fly'.

The look on his face! He hadn't expected my father to say that.

The night he tells his parents I want to dig a hole and jump into it. His mother doesn't approve because we have been 'living in sin' for the last few months. I'm a bad influence on her son. He argues with his mother in the kitchen while I sit with his deaf father in the lounge room and try to make polite conversation.

C:> Ctrl S, 5

I want to speed it up until I get to the wedding — to see my mother again. She will die shortly after our wedding and I wanted to imprint her face on my memory as it was on that day: alive and radiant. Photos have faded with time. *She's wearing a golden dress, her eyes sparkle with tears while her mouth is laughing.*

C:> Pause
Pause/Break

Our honeymoon: rain follows us up the coast and when we turn to come home it follows us back again. It always rains when we have holidays.

We live in an old weatherboard house on a farm at Menangle. I'm doing my Diploma of Education by correspondence. My husband's mother asked him to give her back the car she gave him for his twenty-first birthday. Transport is a problem. It's a lonely life for me and I watch daytime television every day.

I'm pregnant and healthy.

*** ERROR ***

Press ESC for exit or SPACE to continue

The screen goes black. This computer seems to have a mind of its own. Everything has been going nicely and it has just stopped.

C:> F1/Help.

*** ERROR ***

*** Please enter new date: dd/mm/yy ***

I know what the computer is wanting. I type in the date of my mother's death.

C:> DATE: 12/08/72

C:> TIME: 20:10

We are watching television on our mattress on the floor when the phone rings. My husband answers it. I struggle onto my feet, feeling like a balloon on two sticks. Phone calls in the evening are rare and I sense something is wrong.

He hangs up the phone and comes toward me, hands outstretched. 'That was your uncle on the phone. Your mother has had a fatal asthma attack.'

It takes a moment for the word 'fatal' to make sense. This is a shock — my thinking is not fuddled. I'm strong enough to handle it. My mind races through a dozen practical issues: Dad — I must get to him; I'm seven months pregnant — a shock like this could bring the baby early. I pack my hospital bag. What about my brothers? How will they cope if I have to go into hospital? We pack the car and are on our way to my parents' house in Sydney. On the way we buy a bottle of scotch.

We enter the house. In the kitchen on the fridge door is a note from my mother to my fourteen-year-old brother. It gives him instructions on how to feed himself for the day and ends with these words: 'See you tonight, Love Mum'. I put the note in my purse because I don't want anyone else to see it. Later I flush it down the toilet.

BECAUSE IT'S WRONG!

She wasn't there. She didn't come home.

My father is standing by the heater, shivering. He can't stop shivering.

My uncle explains. They were out with my parents during the day and on the way home my mother stopped breathing. She was dead on arrival at the hospital.

I turn away from the computer and surrender to grief. She never saw her grandchildren.

When I return to the monitor, I am prompted for a new date.

C:> DATE: 22/10/73

I'm in labour. My legs in stirrups, my husband is telling me to push. They're telling me it has red hair and having bets about its sex. My father pokes his head in the door and they shoo him out. When they place the screaming male child on my stomach I howl; we are a mother and son chorus.

I have post-natal blues and my father visits me. He tells me he is going overseas and wants me to look after my young brother — just in case anything happens to him. My father tells me he can't live without my mother. I'm overwhelmed with motherhood and I tell him I can't and I won't look after my brother. My father and my brother travel together and return together.

C:> Pause

Pause/Break

I feel emotionally drained and decide to speed up the action until the birth of my second son.

C:> Ctrl S, 9

C:> DATE: 11/03/75, Ctrl S, 1

I'm in labour again but there have been complications with this pregnancy. I've been in hospital for a month after haemorrhaging with a suspected placenta praevia. Everything is happening so fast I have no control. There's only one nurse — she doesn't know where the doctor is and she keeps sticking her head out the door, calling for help. I'm lying on my side and I'm supposed to be doing my rapid breathing but I can't concentrate. I feel the tearing and can't stop the screaming. The nurse swears and turns me over onto my back. The baby's head is between my legs and his little body slips out.

I'm not allowed to hold him. There are more nurses here now. They think he's got concussion and they take him away. There's a lot of blood and they are examining the placenta.

Later, when I'm given my healthy son to nurse, they tell me that it was just as well I only took twenty minutes or they would have been delivering babies in the corridor. It had been a busy day in a sleepy country town hospital.

C:> Ctrl S, 9

The years of early motherhood were fulfilling. I let them drift away. I completed my studies with small children around my ankles and became a qualified English/History teacher. I hated teaching and looked forward to moving to Adelaide where my husband's career thrived.

I worked with him when we set up an office in Adelaide and later after the children started school. I made lifelong friends in Adelaide and was devastated when we returned to Sydney five years later.

Sydney was cold and expensive. It was tempting to rush through these years but I thought there might be some value in reminding myself.

C:> Ctrl S, 5

We can't afford this house in Hunters Hill. We have an enormous bank loan at high interest and I am scraping for enough cash to feed and clothe the family.

While living so comfortably in Adelaide we'd accumulated more furniture than would fit in this house and it's a mess. My youngest is phobic about his wardrobe and won't open it because he's convinced it contains some sort of monster. He hates school and comes home in tears. I have an argument with his form mistress — she is keeping him in after school because of his handwriting. I ask her if she's ever heard of 'positive reinforcement' (buzz words from my teaching days) and she tells me I'm a neurotic, over-protective mother. My oldest is being picked on by bullies and gets bitten on the bottom by a neighbour's dog.

I have to register my car and get lost trying to find a non-one-way street that will take me to the motor registry. I have a panic attack and decide I can't drive in this city. I shut myself up in the house and avoid people. I'm jealous of my husband's work which keeps him away from home and leaves me alone to cope with the kids, the shopping and Sydney traffic.

My son sees a counsellor for his wardrobe phobia and builds a cubby on top of it. His handwriting never improves but he's good at maths. I see a shrink for treatment for my panic attacks.

C:> Ctrl S, 9

I decide to speed up the next few years, which seem less important now. I eventually settle in Sydney. I reconsider teaching but chicken out and go back to university for a few years where I make some friends. I don't finish my studies. Instead I set up a small business, start writing in my spare time and find life is generally busy and rewarding — until May 1991.

I understand the way this computer thinks now and I know it won't let me skip this crisis.

C:> Pause

Pause/Break

Through the window I can see the sun is nudging the horizon. I make a cup of coffee and wander around the house while I drink it. It's a larger house than our first house here in Sydney and has a northern aspect and views. I enjoy living here. Now I feel brave enough to go back to the computer.

C:> Ctrl S, 1

My husband is getting angina. He's only forty-five, has an important position in head office in Sydney and is highly motivated to succeed. We see doctors who tell us that they'd like to treat it with medication. It's not operable, they say. No surgeon is keen to do a bypass. He takes pills, gives up smoking, watches his diet, but the chest pains continue.

He takes Anginine when it's bad. He has to take Anginine while he's getting dressed. I suggest he take a day off. He says it's only indigestion. We try walking the dog, but he gets more pain and takes another Anginine. I get him home and say I'm ringing the doctor. He says he's got an important meeting and he feels all right now. He drives off.

I ring the doctor who tells me I shouldn't have let him go to work. The doctor wants me to get him to a hospital. I ring him on the car phone and he tells me that I'm being ridiculous. Then I get a phone call from his work. He's not well, say his colleagues. He's very pale. He drives home after swallowing more Anginine. He's lost count of how many he's taken.

The doctor sends him to hospital. From his hospital bed he dictates notes to me that I go home, type up and fax to relevant people. They're trying to stabilise him but his angina increases.

He's sent downstairs for an angiogram. He has a massive attack and they put him into intensive care. Cardiac surgery first thing in the morning.

The doctor sees me. 'There's no guarantees,' he says. 'His condition is theoretically inoperable, but he'll not leave hospital without a bypass. Your children should come and see their father tonight. They may not have another opportunity.'

My eldest son prays, my youngest cries. My husband's mother is confused; my father-in-law died three years ago and this is not the way it should be. I won't leave his side. My father comes and takes me home for a few hours.

My dead father-in-law visits my husband while he is unconscious. He's in a rowboat and my husband is drowning in the ocean. *His father refuses to help him into the boat. He tells him to go back and it's a long swim.*

'*His arteries are awful.*' Doctors, talking about my husband. '*I would have liked to do six but I could only do four.*' He's had a quadruple bypass and he's alive. '*He'll need medication for the rest of his life, but he should enjoy a reasonable quality of life.*'

C:> Pause

Pause/Break

Through the window I see birds fly across the horizon in the slanting rays of the sun. I hear an alarm clock in my twenty-one-year-old son's bedroom. A door slams. A toilet flushes.

I don't want to stop but I must get them breakfasted and off to work. I push the on/off switch on the monitor so the screen dies, although the computer is still on. I'll come back to it later.

I bring a cup of coffee to my husband in bed, as I often do in the morning.

'Where've you been?' he asks.

'I couldn't sleep. I was doing some writing,' I lie, but resolve to confess to the night's activities after I finish the game. I climb under the bedclothes and he holds my hand and gives it a squeeze.

'I'm sorry about last night,' he says.

For a moment I'm confused, then I remember the argument between my husband and my sons. It seems so trivial. 'It's okay,' I assure him. 'I guess it's normal for fathers and sons to fight.'

At breakfast my two sons are also apologetic.

'I'm making a resolution,' says my twenty-one-year-old. 'No more computer games. They're addictive and I've got to focus on my studies or I won't get through this year.'

'I'm sorry I brought that game home,' said my nineteen-year-old. 'I'm going to delete it from the computer before I go to work.'

'No, don't do that,' I say, a note of panic in my voice. Three astonished men look at me and I blush. 'The truth is, I've been playing that game and I haven't finished it yet.'

'I don't believe this!' says twenty-one-year-old. 'Mum? Playing a computer game?'

We all go into the study and I position myself in front of the monitor. I push the on/off button on the monitor. I can see a road leading to some place off the screen.

'Looks like you've only just started,' says nineteen-year-old.

'Oh, no, I haven't,' I tell him. 'And I've got a long way to go yet.' I can feel the warmth of their bodies behind me, my husband's hands on my shoulders. What will happen to us in the future? I love them so much it's tempting to continue the game past the present, but I'm frightened. I can't do it. I stand up on shaking legs and let them take over the keyboard. 'You're right,' I say in my brightest voice. 'I think you should delete it.' After all, I don't understand anything about computers.

However, I want to tell them that I do know something about life. It's not a game and you only have one of them. I was pleased to see that the end of the road in my game was some place off the screen and I had no desire to continue playing until I could see it.

A LIFE

Anneliese Stricker

She was born in April 1910 in Germany's Ruhr district. She had little babyhood; two brothers were born within two years. She had a dolls' house, fully furnished — she loved it dearly — made by her police sergeant father. Her town, more like a village really, was not obviously industrial. There were coal mines — she was not permitted to speak to the miners' children — but the town was more rural than urban. Her parents rented a house on the edge of the village opposite a farm. Her mother made preserves for winter from produce grown in the garden. Other produce was stored in the cellar. There was plenty to eat, winter and summer. At Easter her father took her walking in the woods, to find painted eggs left by the Easter hare.

In 1914 her father went to war. In 1918 he returned from Russia. While he was away there was less to eat. After his return he beat her mother: there was talk that she had acted immorally with a lodger. Her father also beat his children. The years of beatings outnumbered those of war. On Sundays the family went to mass at St Agathe's. The girl liked to put field flowers on the grave of the baby sister born before her conception.

In 1918 the victorious armies imposed a blockade on Germany and food was scarce. Her father guarded his garden with a rifle. They hid a pig, for fattening, in the cellar.

When the knife slit its throat it screamed. The blood pudding was very good.

By 1919 she was luminously fair, high-cheekboned, a dreamer. With her best friend, eldest of the neighbouring farmer's three children, she played games involving sainthood. Both wished to be nuns. They deliciously mortified their flesh with candle flames and the thorns of wild roses. During the communist uprising, when their town was a battleground, they were Red Cross nurses in the boys' games of *Kommunisten und Reichswehr.* Her sympathies were with the *Kommunisten.*

In January 1923 French troops occupied her town: something to do with default in deliveries of coal for war reparations. Frenchmen 'requisitioned' the produce of vegetable plots and farms. Inflation caused by German and Allied government policies made the town's women take wheelbarrows to their husbands' places of work twice daily to collect wages. A barrowload of paper currency bought half a loaf of bread. Turnips grown secretly, among weeds, were the family's staple food. She and her brothers daily searched the wood for berries, nuts and herbs to supplement the turnips. They were beaten if they failed to collect enough.

Also in 1923 wealthy conservatives, middle-class Germans and Austrians, devised a scheme through the Pan-German movement to send poor German children to cultured Austrian Catholic families for a year, and vice versa. The town schoolteacher, aware of beatings that scarred two of his pupils, arranged their participation. She was sent to Vienna, her brother elsewhere. At the railway station her mother kissed her for the first time.

In Vienna she found music, poetry, art; experienced loving kindness. After her return her father said as he beat her, 'Vienna ruined you.'

In 1925 her mother died of 'a woman's complaint' and her father remarried. The children called their stepmother the *Eisheilige*, the Ice-saint. The Ice-saint had connections with a renowned Prussian order of nuns.

In 1926 she was sent to the Prussian convent as a charity student. For two years she learned household management: cleaning, nursing — the convent had a hospital for the tuberculous — bookkeeping, sewing, cooking. The daughters of the wealthy were taught finer skills. She planned to be a nun, serve in darkest Africa. She was ostracised for three months for discussing the nature of the Holy Trinity. She wrote poems, secretly sent them to a newspaper. The editor sent her red roses. She was expelled. The Ice-saint refused to have her in the house.

1928 was not a good year for finding work in Germany. To her puzzlement many prospective employers asked her to take off her clothes. After living on three sugar lumps stolen from pavement cafés and one bread roll a day, she did so. This act led to work in a Rhineland orchard, cooking and cleaning for field workers during the day and packers at night. The orchardist and his son fought drunkenly for her favours. She loathed both, left, found a series of menial jobs by the legendary river and became feverishly moody.

In 1931 she returned to Vienna, seeking work and past dreams. She was unaware that in this city of *Gemütlichkeit* corpses of the starved were still collected daily. Booking a train ticket to Germany at the Westbahnhof, she was approached by a mature, polished man of Jewish appearance.

'Madame,' he said, bowing over her hand, 'it is my birthday and I am alone. Would you do me the honour of accompanying me to the theatre? We could first dine at Sacher's.' Perhaps the latter was the attraction for her. After the theatre they went to his inner-city rooms. She was impressed by the brass plate: *Rechtsanwald*, lawyer. She slept in his bed, he on a velvet ottoman in his office. The next day they travelled to the Attersee, a charming alpine lake. Here they did not sleep separately. He proposed, she accepted, only later learning he proposed to all women.

She became feverish and they consulted a physician: she had tuberculosis and returned to Germany, where her health insurance was valid, for two years' treatment. He wrote daily, sent roses to the sanatorium three times a week. That her atheistic, intellectual fiancé was Jewish did not trouble her. She formally renounced Catholicism.

In 1933, the year of Hitler's election, they married in Vienna. Her sister-in-law asked, 'Do you know what you are doing, marrying him?' The bride was unaware of the groom's emotional instability and thus the question's meaning. Treatment of her tuberculosis continued.

By 1935, her lungs healed, she realised she detested her husband and knew she expected his child. Again they slept separately, a pattern that became permanent. Her daughter was born, genetically flawed, in 1936. Her screams as she expelled it reminded her of her father's pig, his words about Vienna. She felt ruined.

In 1938 screaming crowds welcomed Hitler to Vienna. Seyss-Inquart, Austria's new Nazi governor, warned her husband, a legal colleague, of impending arrest. They fled to Haiti, the only place for which her husband's bribery secured visas. She wondered why she went with him. A sense of sacrifice? Hatred of German authority? The island was unhealthy, the flawed child often ill. Her husband failed in businesses undertaken while awaiting further visas. He had applied to sixteen countries for entry. Only Australia replied.

On 29 April 1939 the family arrived in Sydney. Their total assets were seven hundred pounds; the Australian government required refugee Jews to have this sum so there would be no drain on a state that was still in depression. Her chief assets were her beauty and convent-learned skills.

On 9 May 1939 she found work, and accommodation for herself and her daughter, cooking at a Blue Mountains home for mentally deficient and emotionally disturbed children. Drought, dust and bushfire horrified her more than did the children. Her husband, refused army enlistment, briefly sold encyclopaedias, they bought a western suburbs ham-and-beef shop with accommodation above. On 29 May she joined him, leaving her child, temporarily, at the school for the disturbed. A shop and dwelling that needed so much scrubbing was no place for a child. When she had time to feel, the child's absence gouged her heart.

Early in September 1939 she reclaimed her daughter. Next day World War II was declared. Anti-foreigner feeling ensured business failure. She bitterly blamed her husband: 'You, with your university degrees, your intellectual pretensions. You are a failure. Everything you touch fails.'

In October they bought a shop in King's Cross and found a small flat nearby. Her husband walked to and from the morning markets: trams did not run so early. In a rucksack and two suitcases he carried freshly killed carcasses of chickens and rabbits. She plucked, skinned, cleaned and cooked them, along with brawns, patés, soups and roast meats. She made salads previously unknown in this land of exile. She also kept the books. 'It is ironic that my misery in the convent now supports us,' she said.

She and her husband served customers in the shop. Their child was minded by an old woman — later dismissed for drunkenness — or played among crates behind the shop. The couple's combined daily working hours far exceeding twenty-four; the shop was closed only on Christmas Day and Easter Sunday. For Easter she painted eggs, hid them in little nests to delight her child.

Once a week, for a shilling, she went to the newsreel theatrette, her only entertainment. Here she saw footage of Hitler. She wept and told her friend at the Arabian coffee shop next door, 'I vent to ze pictures and bloody upset myself.'

'A lady doesn't say that,' her friend said.

'Please, I am sorry, I learn only.'

'Lady, if you're only learning,' said a passing soldier, 'what'll you be like in a year?'

In June 1940 Italy entered the war. Her husband again tried to enlist. They were declared enemy aliens; their wireless and camera were impounded. She needed a police permit to take her child to play in a nearby park. To the tune of a popular song she sang, 'South of the Border, down Rushcutter's Bay.'

She was beaten senseless by an Australian neighbour who had previously pawed her: 'Go back where you came from, Nazi German Jew!'

The shop was closed by order. Money melted like the ice in the cool-chests. About to sell the shop, she was stopped by a friendly policeman addicted to her food and beauty. 'The ban'll be lifted next week,' he mumbled through her metwurst.

Spent, she sent her four-year-old to boarding school. Parting brought intense pain. She brought her home, malnourished, seven months later.

In December 1941 Pearl Harbor brought American servicemen to Sydney and increased sales to the shop. She employed staff.

In January 1942 love lit up her life for the first time. The Allied victory of Tobruk flung a shell-shocked Rat into her shop, heart and (while her husband worked his shift) bed. The victorious young soldier, sick in soul and body, was healed by the balm of her love. The child was boarded at Santa Sabina. Too soon, the soldier was posted north, fought on the Kokoda Track. She illegally aborted a pregnancy. Husband and wife moved to cheaper accommodation to afford the fees for abortion and boarding school. Kokoda's aftermath brought soldier, but not child, back to her.

Throughout 1943 she worked the shop without her husband. Now she marketed, cooked, served, was there to clean and close the shop at midnight. He, his enlistment now accepted and barrack-based, cleaned army latrines. She planned a more permanent separation, a plan sabotaged by exhaustion and her daughter's near-mortal illnesses in 1944.

'Think of the child,' her husband said. At year's end she returned the child to the nuns.

On 9 May 1945 victory in Europe was celebrated. On that day she had a hysterectomy. The doctor spoke words she did not understand, something about inflammation from earlier trauma. The shop was sold.

In August 1945 the war ended. Soldier and husband were both demobilised. Feeling sexless, she severed her relationship with the soldier. Muted marital war continued. The child, now nine, came home, became her confidant, her confessor, her reason for living. The child adored her wonderful, sad mother.

The Nuremberg war crimes trials began.

In February 1946 the couple, partnered by a fellow refugee, opened a dressmaking establishment. Again, her convent-learned skills were useful.

On 8 March 1946 Sydney newspapers carried headlines: 'Sydney Man's War Crime Defence Affidavit'. Her husband had told the Nuremberg Tribunal of Seyss-Inquart's life-saving interventions on their behalf — nevertheless the Nazi governor was hanged. After initial abuse, no member of the refugee community spoke to them again. The partner in the dressmaking venture withdrew funding. Her husband, broken, took work as a country commercial traveller. She felt strangely free, powerful. She *would* succeed.

But in 1947 a Christmas car accident — her husband drove — hospitalised her for a year. She boarded the shaken child with various acquaintances. It took her a further two years to recover finances and physical health.

In the spring of 1950 the soldier, now a communist waterside worker, came to her suggesting marriage. He was wanted by the police for waterfront disturbances. In December she left her husband. He died on 21 January 1951; the certificate stated 'wilful self-strangulation'. She felt strangling guilt. The child, now adolescent, said, 'I'm not sorry. I hated him for what he did to you.' This comforted her.

She sold the business to pay her dead husband's debts, worked as a waitress, later manager, in a well-known coffee-house chain. The owner, enamoured of her elegance and efficiency, raised her wages. The communist asked for money to pay for another woman's abortion. She terminated the relationship. Her daughter gave comfort: 'You're lovely, still young. There'll be others.'

There were. One left her, unable to fill the well of her longing for reassurance and unquestioning love. One offered marriage, a house by the river in Brisbane. He was already married. She left his house when, psychotic, he threatened her life. She returned to Sydney, worked as a housekeeper for wealthy Vaucluse Jews.

In 1953 her daughter also left her. But politely, to become a nurse, then to travel. Communication was frequent, appeared affectionate.

In 1957 she was offered the post of personal assistant to a steel merchant who had known her husband in Vienna. She ran the Sydney end of his business when he visited his London headquarters and home-counties wife. The high-rise building boom boosted sales. With his low-interest loan she bought a house in which she relocated his office. Rent for the office soon paid out the loan. She elegantly entertained his clients, enjoyed position and respect.

'She's wonderful,' people said. She was not convinced.

In 1963 she overdosed when the steel merchant's unwillingness to leave his wife became inescapably clear. She wrote to her daughter, 'I am old, alone, will die soon. I am so weary of life.' She was fifty-three. The daughter returned, lived with her, visited her in private psychiatric hospitals, but left her three years later to pursue a differently dependent life.

She took up pottery, had successful exhibitions. Money thus made was donated to charitable causes, UNICEF, the RSPCA.

In 1967 she retired from the steel firm after the merchant's death by carbon monoxide poisoning. A small golden handshake supplemented her widow's pension. A late love affair — her beauty was still luminous — ended when a heart attack killed her lover. She sought reassurance.

'Am I evil?' she asked. 'Everyone I love deserts me.'

Some years later she complained to her daughter of the difficulties of maintaining a large house and garden.

'I am wretched,' she said. 'I rattle around in this cavern I can no longer cope with. There are so many bad memories here. My health suffers.' She had a heart condition, frail bones — her ribs had fractured in falls. She bought a house in the inner-west harbourside suburb where her daughter lived, divided it into two side-by-side flats, invited her daughter to use one at a fair rental.

Together they lived their separate lives. She daily spoke of her memories of use and abuse. She spoke also of her imminent death.

'You will be well off when I die,' she always said. The daughter had a breakdown, recovered, left her for a healthier life in the country.

After recovering from the rage of abandonment she told her daughter, 'I am happy that you can make a life for yourself. Mine will soon end.'

She travelled, loved Japan, hated Germany. 'They are all fat peasants. They say they didn't know. I am sure my brother was a Nazi.'

Austria was as bad. 'The charm is all artificial. Vienna is

still the most anti-semitic city in Europe. They paint swastikas on Jewish gravestones.'

In the 1980s she joined the local branch of an anti-nuclear group, became an office bearer, enjoyed the regard of others for her efficiency and verve. 'Your mother is a marvel,' they told the visiting daughter. The branch and its social life ended with the collapse of communism.

She loved her daughter avidly, looked forward eagerly to weekly telephone calls, twice-yearly visits. All she had suffered was worthwhile if her daughter loved her. By the fifth day of each visit she had a migraine, her heart thumped irregularly. But the second week she sobbed, 'You do not love me. All I want is a little love. Is that so much to ask?' She sensed that her daughter itched to leave.

Finding herself arid, she took up environmental causes, saved water, recycled.

In 1994 her secret hope became reality; her daughter returned to the harbourside suburb. Rented a room, began to write a book.

'What is it about?' she asked.

'The effect of history on everyday lives. Relationships. Us,' said the daughter.

'You've left it late. I shall soon be dead.'

The research interviews were painful. *Those who question me are against me,* she thought. She reiterated her sorrows, her longing for love.

Shortly after the interviews began she told her daughter, 'I have decided to end my life at Christmas. It is only fair that you have a little life without me. The house will fetch four hundred thousand. I ask only that you do not plan a Christmas vacation. I want you with me. I have stopped taking my medications and feel very calm.' The interviews would be finished by Christmas, they would be her penultimate gift to her daughter. The daughter pointed out that six months was a long time to be without medication. Two weeks later, ill, she saw this was so.

She was shocked when her daughter accepted an invitation to Canada the following year. Again she decided to end her life. This time she would sell the house, give the daughter the money. Property values were rising as Sydney prepared for the Olympic Games. She arranged an auction, stopped medication. She howled with pain when her daughter appeared ungrateful.

'I cannot understand why you force me to continue my miserable life!' she cried.

'I cannot understand why you must sell your house in order to die,' said the ungrateful daughter. The auction was cancelled.

She took out a loan, the house as security, repayment of capital to come from the estate. Taking her cleaning-woman as companion, she flew to a reefed island. The sea did not soothe her.

'You're wonderful. I love you more than I ever loved my mother,' the cleaning-woman told her.

She wonders why she does not feel content.

SMALL-EYE

Ba Phillips

It was Frankie who first told me about the snake.

'Guess what John's given her. For a present. Go on, guess.' I knew it wasn't a ring. Or a black nightie. So I just said, 'What?'

'A snake. He's given her a snake.' When I didn't say anything, he said, 'What do you think of that, eh? Barb? Is that natural? When you give your girlfriend a present it's jewellery, or chocolates.'

I said at last, 'She hated chocolates, you know that.'

He laughed. 'Yeah. He did bring her chocolate biscuits and she didn't like them, so she gave them to me.'

'Well,' I said, 'he finally got the message.'

'But a snake? Is that natural? Come on, Barb, you're a woman. Would you like a snake?'

When I told Patricia about the snake she said, 'Oh, that makes me feel quite sick.'

'But John's a nature lover. Don't forget that.' I was grappling with it.

Frankie said she wrote to him about it, saying she didn't know what she was supposed to do with a snake, especially since John was off again, doing 'things'. I thought about where the snake would be. Not inside, surely; I imagined it must be a carpet snake, but then I thought of the carpet snakes of my childhood, the big ones they kept in the local produce store. Remember those places? That smell? They had great bags of grain and potatoes. People like my grandmother used to go there and get big orders which were delivered. My grandmother used to have a lot of chooks and a cow named Trixie, so I suppose she needed produce to feed them. It wasn't unlike the smell of manure, come to think of it, though drier. It made me sneeze.

It isn't like that now where I live in the city, but Annie didn't live in the city any more. She lived in the country, in a small backwater called Redhead out of Taree. She was a city girl, London, south-east I think her brother Raymond said. Not quite Cockney, but nearly. They were poor when Annie and Raymond were little; she often told me about it. 'Old knickers,' she used to say; when she went to the grammar school her knickers, all her uniform, were not as new and swish as the other girls'.

'That's because our father was useless,' she said. 'He didn't earn anything and he drank everything that our mother earned. He even pinched the shillings from the gas meter so when it was cold we had no heating. I nearly died once because of that,' she said, tossing her dark head. It was in a bob, the side bits longer than the back.

The point about it being a carpet snake is that they are quite friendly but they eat mice and rats. That's what they were for in the produce store. But Annie's house was a duplex and very new. She seemed to be camping in it, as there wasn't much there — a few things like posters on the wall and a settee with lots of cushions, all in different Indian designs. She got rid of most of her stuff when she went to Istanbul about three years ago. She certainly hadn't got mice or rats. She kept the house very clean, and had the English obsession about getting her place regularly redecorated. I think it's the English obsession; my family never did it. Her real house, the only thing she owned, was a little cottage in Glebe. Since she had known John it had developed a garden, and Annie also had the kitchen and bathroom done. She had an affair with the builder too. There might have been a few rats around Glebe, but not enough to keep a carpet snake happy, I would have thought. I pondered over this.

While I was in the train going up to Newcastle to see her in the John Hunter Hospital, which looks like a ship with big funnels everywhere, probably for the air-conditioning, I thought about the snake. Sarah had said it must have been the Goddess. She didn't laugh or look surprised when I told her about the snake, but nodded rather mysteriously.

'The Goddess?' I said. 'Annie was always on about her Goddess.'

'Well there you are,' she said. 'It was what the Goddess needed. That's why snakes have always had such bad press; they go with the Goddess.'

'In the Garden of Eden —' I began.

'Yes. That's why a perfectly nice animal like a snake was suddenly identified with evil. Because the men wanted to outlaw the Goddess. *She* was what they saw as evil, not the snake.'

'Oh,' I said, doubtfully. I didn't think John knew this. I must ask him I thought, when I get there. At the John Hunter Hospital.

When I arrived, Annie was in a coma in intensive care. She looked very still except for the regular breathing provided by the ventilator near her. I felt a rush of warmth in my mouth and tasted salt. Mark told me to bear up and be cheerful. He was her tenant in the house in Glebe, an actor who had done the Ensemble Theatre acting course with Annie years ago. He is a big bloke with a nice big voice, lowered gently, and was brought up a Catholic. He is in his middle age somewhere; perhaps forties or even fifties. Annie and I are; when they guessed her age as she was admitted they reckoned thirty-six. She would have loved that. She was little and neat-bodied, not scrawny, well covered though slender. Lovely really. Dark hair, rather long lately. 'I think I'll have a little foray into floozy, Barb,' she said breezily. It had been giving her a bit of trouble until she found out that rosemary was good for dry hair. When I went to stay with her at Redhead, she smelled strongly of rosemary. Could have had her with roast potatoes and lamb.

Everyone in intensive care was gloomy about Annie. They were talking of turning the machine off from the first. When the helicopter pilot came in, Narelle the nurse told me not to hope. The pilot was not the one who had airlifted her from the scene of the accident; this was another guy, a born-again who came in on his day off to pray for her.

'Do you mind if I pray for her?' he said. He was quite a scrummy-looking guy so I thought Annie wouldn't mind. He bent over her and whispered in her ear.

He said, 'Ann, Ann — I want to pray for you. Do you understand?'

He was practically kissing her right ear.

The nurses told us to talk to her because she might be able to hear. We did anyway; you have to. We took her hand and stroked her arm. When she sort of came to, in the second week, we noticed that she was irritated by this stroking and pulled away. This thrilled me. She hated being pawed unless she was being made love to; all the people coming up to visit had her at their mercy. She couldn't stop them pawing her and talking to her. It was an irony because she'd gone to Taree to escape. Well, at least she was pulling away. They said she was still in the coma, but she couldn't have been, could she? Not if she pulled away.

The helicopter pilot prayed quite softly but I could hear him telling her that by the love and strength of our Lord Jesus Christ she was well again. Then he stood up, smiled at me and said she was cured. Narelle frowned at the machine. When he left, I bent over Annie and said it didn't matter whether it was JC, the Goddess or Mickey Mouse, as long as she was going to get better.

Narelle shook her head. 'I must ask you not to put too much faith in — that man,' she said. 'He means well, but Ann is very, very gravely ill. I hope you understand that.'

They said it often enough, the people in intensive care. We understood they weren't hoping, even if we were. I never saw Narelle again; I think it was their policy to change their staff all the time to avoid their getting involved with the patients. How cruel, what strange nursing. Not like the old days when there weren't any machines. One of the Taree teachers who used to be a nurse said the nurses saw themselves as technicians now.

John still hadn't been contacted. Annie had been driving down to Sydney to do some marking and a staff development course. South of Bulahdelah, she had stopped at a 'Stop' lollipop held aloft by a guy in a road gang, but the gent behind had not noticed her stopping, apparently, and ploughed into her. The ganger leapt away nimbly, narrowly escaping Annie's car. The inattentive driver and his passengers were slightly injured, but Annie had a massive wallop to the left side of her skull behind the left ear, and spinal damage as we later found out.

She was said to have spoken after the accident but this later seemed to be a furphy. One of her mates in Taree had been speaking to the man next door, a road worker, who had heard it from one of the gang on the scene. She was supposed to have said, 'I heard a click.' I thought it was interesting because when I fell on the stony bed of the creek at my sister's place just after being diagnosed with multiple myeloma, I heard my wrist click. It was fractured. My doctor had said to avoid fractures because multiple myeloma is a disease of the bone marrow. Bugger it, I thought. But it all turned out okay and the fracture healed well.

I'm just clumsy in stony creek beds. Not like Annie,

who was never clumsy. She told me tenderly once she'd noticed I was clumsy when on uneven ground. 'Not otherwise, Barb,' she said sweetly. 'Just when you have to negotiate a bit.' Her back gate was on uneven ground and she used to put a hand out to steady me.

She always had a good sense of balance; that's why she was such a good dancer. She talked me into going belly dancing in the Orange Grove public school every Thursday night. She was better than I was, though I dressed up more. The first night they thought I was the teacher, I was so tarted up. Annie had always danced a lot, semi-professionally too, and was very light.

We both adored the teacher who was as slim as a snake and very ethereal; her boyfriend used to come along and smooch with her before the class, and if you came early you'd catch them. It was lovely. Annie would say, 'It makes me come over all warm and damp, Barb,' and I would agree with her.

We agreed on lots of things. Once I wrote to her while she was in Istanbul that the great consolation of my life was pretty things; she brought me back a large turquoise oval which I had made into an earring. The prettiest thing. I've got it on, now.

John couldn't be contacted at first because ... well, John is unusual. He's an Aquarian and he is often uncontactable. It drove Annie mad. 'Is there any point?' she would say. 'Is there any *point*?' She told me endlessly they were from different worlds; he seemed unable to see that she wanted to meet his friends, be taken out.

'Is that so amazing?' she'd say. 'I just want to go out to coffee, sit on the footpath at a little table with an umbrella, talk. *Why* can't he? Am I so plain he's ashamed to be seen with me?' And so on.

Naturally Annie was not plain. She was vibrant. Like a lovely little high-stepping horse, a filly. Her maiden name was Feehelly. Just like filly, don't you think? But she was fifteen years older than John. Did this have any bearing on it? I don't know. When she was dying, someone mentioned her age and I looked quickly at John, stroking her forehead, and murmuring. He smiled at me. 'Did you think I didn't know, Barb?' he said, his blue round eyes temporarily merry.

'I — told them not to tell you just in case,' I muttered.

'I knew,' he said.

Annie was in a deep coma again after three days of freedom and her head was swollen with the secondary haemorrhage. They had shaved off her long hair. Where I was sitting the wound looked big and ugly, fastened together in huge untidy stitches behind her ear. Her face was smooth and creamy with two red channels running down the side of her mouth. She had the tubes out of her throat and a tracheotomy inserted in her neck. I said brightly, 'What about this present John's supposed to have given you? Is it true he's given you a snake? That's a bit Freudian isn't it, eh?'

Raymond, Annie's little brother, began to laugh and John joined in.

'Okay, John,' I said, 'what kind of snake? You'd better come clean and tell us all about it.'

His pointed teeth showed as he grinned. '*What* about it?'

'Well, what kind of snake is it? Is it a carpet snake?'

He shook his head. He glanced quickly at Annie and smoothed the space between her eyes.

'It's a black snake,' he said. Really he whispered. He speaks very softly. Sometimes you have to lean over to hear him.

'But they're venomous,' I said. 'Not the red-bellied black snake?' My sister has hundreds of them at her place. When you disturb them, they rear up like forked silver, catching the light.

'No. It's called the small-eyed black snake.' Raymond

and I laughed loudly. I suppose we were reminded of the one-eyed trouser snake.

'But *why*, John? Why a snake?' I really did want to know. He just said very quietly that he hoped to give her a close encounter of an unusual kind. And then of course I realised; it was simple. John is a nature man. He goes bush and he finds things like small-eyed black snakes as he's walking along. He put this one in a bag and brought it to show Annie.

'Where is it now?' I asked.

'Redhead,' said John.

He explained it was in a drum in the back yard, near the paddock where the horses were. We'd talked to these horses when I stayed with Annie. They were very white-eyed. John said Annie was captivated when she found out they lay down to sleep with their legs sticking out. I was, too; I hadn't known horses lay down to sleep. I asked John whether anyone was feeding Small-Eye. He explained snakes don't eat every day.

'What about exercise? Can it run about?' I asked, anxiously.

'He is lying peacefully in his drum,' he said. 'It's like a log. He doesn't run about much at any time. He just lies waiting for his prey in his log.'

'Prey? What, rats?'

'Frogs. Skinks. Whatever comes along.'

I thought about it and then I said, 'When are you going to let him go?'

He said, 'You don't have to worry about him, Barb. I'll look after him. I'll let him go when I find a good place, where he'll be safe.'

I must have raised my eyebrows because he went on, 'You don't just let a small-eyed black snake out anywhere. It has to be a good place, where there's food, and privacy. For him.'

When Frankie rang up, finally, I told him there was

nothing sinister about Small-Eye. Frank was sceptical. He was perhaps a little jealous of John. He wanted to love Annie the most and have her love him the most. He said he hadn't come up straight away because he couldn't bear to see her dying. He'd met her when he was fifteen — seven years ago — at the Ensemble and they'd hidden in the dunny to avoid a dance class taken by No-Knickers Helen. Annie was a sort of Auntie Mame to Frankie; he loved her. He's gay and pretty and I think at some level he wants to *be* her. They were kind to each other. When she wept over John, Frank wanted to protect her. Well, we all did, of course. But from what?

She fancied him, that was clear. We talked about it end-lessly on the phone, having no men of mine to discuss; I have retired from all that. I used to say I was a born-again virgin, but now I think retired heterosexual is the better term; the former is too challenging. I suppose we wanted to save Annie the pain of love while knowing how puerile this is. Love is pain when he's fifteen years younger and you don't meet his friends. It is. Annie thought it was.

My sister is married to a much younger man, and she's much younger than me. When I show people his photo in his sailor uniform, they say, 'Your *brother-in-law?*' My sister and Annie were right, though; the elderly dick can be tricky. Treacherous blokes running out on their old wives and marrying much younger women might say it's the riv-etting personalities that beckon, that the sex is secondary; well, yeah, it sure is. For the younger woman it's tertiary. The first time I saw a fifty-four-year-old dick I was horri-fied. No, I've got nothing against men. You just might as well get a nice fresh one, like a lettuce.

Taree TAFE was better than most, Annie reckoned. The campus was rural and included a herd of dairy cows. Annie liked the way the place was full of dogs, too. The teachers brought them in to work. I think she said there were two bitches called Zoe. She liked looking out of the classroom window and seeing cows and green paddocks. Glebe had been giving her the shits, mainly because of the garbage. 'I've got to get out of the city, Barb,' she said, 'though I've no business leaving you now.'

'I'll come up for visits,' I said. I knew crowding her was no good. Neither was needing her.

'You'll get better,' she said. 'Don't think of dying. I might go out tomorrow and get hit by a bus.'

She wrote to me from Taree that she made no friends and refused all invitations. When she was hit by the car, the friends she had shed all came rushing back; all her Ensemble friends, and her old friends from when she was married, as well as all her TAFE-teacher friends. And lovers. The hospital people were amazed at the deluge of inquiries. And they came too, in droves, to sit at her white bed-for-spinals with all the machines around her, holding her hand and stroking her. Patricia didn't go; she was afraid Annie didn't want to see her. They had fallen out a year ago and Patricia never worked out why. Not up to me to tell her. Annie had pared everything down — things as well as people. She went travelling north lightly.

I never expected her to die. I was the one to die. She was tougher and braver than I am, though she sent me a card for last birthday with *To the bravest gel I know* on it. I asked her about that. Why did she think a wimp like me was brave? I couldn't cheek the bosses the way she did; she was wonderful. I just had a nervous breakdown and got cancer. She laughed and said there were many ways to be brave. When I was looking down at her in that second week in hospital, when she came out of the deep coma for three days, I told her I would be there all through the rehab. I said we would get better together, and that I loved her. There was no one else there that day; we were close. She looked up at me with both eyes focused; it was the first time. I sang to her and read her a poem I'd written in the train; I told her she was pretty and listed all her features. I said she looked like a goddess. Her eyes filled with tears, and when I told Stan the Indian nurse, he said it was probably just moisture collecting. 'No,' I said; 'there's too much. She's weeping.' She couldn't smile because of the tubes down her throat, but sometimes her face flushed red and she moved her mouth as though she were trying to tell me. I told her to have a little zizz, that I would be there when she woke up; like a little obedient dog, she closed her eyes and went to sleep. When she woke up she fixed her eyes on me again, with that open candid sad look. It was a talking look. When I went home on the train I wept quietly to myself, wondering what her eyes meant by that look. Now, I think they meant she was only back for a visit; that she was going and not to stop her. Of course I could be wrong. No one will ever know.

After the three days she had another haemorrhage and the hospital said she would not live. She would be too damaged. They wanted to turn the machine off and Raymond agreed with them. I met John in the corridor. He said she had 'talked' to him just before it happened.

'She told me she wanted to go,' he said in his barely audible voice.

'How?' I said.

'We discussed this a few weeks ago, you know,' he whispered, 'and we said what we wanted to happen.'

'Eh?' I wished he would speak up.

'Yes. In the event of an accident, because she'd just got the car.'

He looked very awry, his long fair hair hanging sadly. I thought he had more wrinkles than she did and his teeth were odd. Pointed. He is a small man and slim; he and Annie were a match size-wise. But his eyes are prominent and blue and he sort of sticks them out, where hers were large and soft and the colour of a pond. You could drown in them, or at least come up with midges in your mouth.

'Oh yes?'

'Well, we decided that neither of us would want to go on half dead; or ...'

I nodded. That's what I would have said too, fit and well; but lying hurt, would you still say that? Is life still sweet at half-throttle? I suppose it's a matter of degree, isn't it? I don't want to die because I'm not as pretty as I was or I can't swim as far or dance as long or get out of a chair as quickly and gracefully. And because I'm alone. That's not enough to die for.

'How did she tell you she still felt the same as when you talked?'

'I asked did she and she blinked, once. We were doing one blink for yes and two for no.'

'Really?' I said. 'Really John?'

And he blinked once, too.

The contents of letters are private, but I can tell you a little of what was in her last letter. It was an angry suffering letter. She was raving about TAFE, which she thought was a sick institution. She raved a little about John, too. She said she didn't know whether he had moved in or not, but that he had paid for the groceries. Her young men usually didn't. She said she wanted to see me, to hear I was better, and that we must get Frankie over and rub up against each other the way wolves do. She knows how crazy for animals I am. One sentence was bad. She said, 'How am I going to get out of TAFE, until I grow my own tumour?'

You know of course that she died. They turned the machine off and she died. Never again regained consciousness, and her head swelled like a cauliflower. It was this that made me frightened when Raymond asked me to do her make-up for the viewing. He wanted a viewing. I couldn't refuse him, but asked that the mortician be there to help me if I couldn't manage it. John came too, and I asked Frankie.

'I can't,' he said.

'Yes,' I corrected him. 'You can. It's not any dead body; it's Annie. And we love her.'

I went over to a mate's garden and picked a lot of big gardenias; there were still heaps of little ones on my bush too. I filled a big box. Frankie brought a bunch of December lilies, pink and white. I took a selection of scarves. When we got there we both made a funny noise in our throats, but held each other's hand until we could get up close. She wasn't bruised and rotting, as somebody had warned me, but creamy and silky, her skin perfect and her eyes not quite closed. The mortician pulled on his gloves and applied the make-up we took out of her little make-up purse. That familiar little purse. We chose a lilac eye-shadow, black mascara and her coral-pink blusher. The pink was just the pink in the chiffon scarf with the cham-pagne fringe. We arranged that around her face, covering the swelling. When he touched up her mouth with the matching coral lipstick, she suddenly looked enticing again, and her eyes just about to open. Then we covered her with flowers, all over her scarf and white satin shroud. The gardenias were near her face and the December lilies lightly resting on her small body. She looked like Persephone ready to wake up. The mortician wheeled her out into the viewing parlour where dreamy music was oozing out of a cassette player. John shot up and said, 'God, I want to kiss her.'

'Goddess,' we murmured, 'goddess.'

He came round last night. It was the hottest December day in Sydney since 1957. I wasn't in Sydney then; I wondered whether Annie was. We talked until one-thirty in the morning and then he went out to his car, with a bag of peaches, to drive up to Redhead and Annie's smell on the bedclothes. I asked him about letting Small-Eye go but he didn't hear me. He'd just told me he blamed the hospital for turning the machine off before she'd had a chance.

'But John,' I said; 'she wanted to go. You told me she wanted to go.'

He looked up from his cold cup of tea. He looked bewildered. 'What?' he said.

I repeated it. 'You told me, at the hospital. She blinked once for yes.'

'No,' he said. 'I never said that.'

He paused and looked at his small brown hands. Snake-catching hands. He was still whispering.

'No. She said nothing. She just looked at me.'

I knew what he meant.

EVENTS IN THE LIFE OF A SIXTEEN-YEAR-OLD ALCOHOLIC

Juliana's story by Mary Devenish

I was born in 1976 in far-west New South Wales to Aboriginal Lorraine O'Shea and Dutch Henry Van Gough. My father was a builder, a good worker, a good money-maker. He usually worked in our district, and sometimes he would travel long distances to be head builder on a project. He always left money in our bank account to take care of us when he was not at home.

I have a brother Willie two years younger than myself. My parents never married. Our family loved to be together. Sometimes Mum and Dad drank too much Dutch gin, laughing and singing, but never fighting. We had a wooden cottage on the outskirts of town. Dad made it beautiful and Mum put white nylon crossover curtains on all the windows.

Grandma Jane and what we call our extended family lived a few miles farther out in the bushland. We'd visit them for picnics, and fishing, and cooking, and mainly for talking. Traditionally black women are storytellers. They hand down oral history. Mothers and grandmothers are strong and have moral courage. We are a spiritual people. From girlhood we face exploitation by males and racial hostility from some whites. We know fear. Some of us have been wanderers from childhood.

Grandma Jane said some white Australian pioneer women possess our qualities as a result of struggle — a hard life.

I went to the nun's school. I started at kindergarten when I was five. Aborigines and half-castes went there as well as whites. There was no discrimination. Dad said my skin was the colour of strong milk coffee and it had the texture of fresh cream. He said I'm his little Dutch queen, that's why he called me Juliana.

When I was seven years old my father left us to go back to Holland. Things were never the same again. Mum began to drink more alcohol, she became sad, melancholy, too depressed to look after Willie and me and our house. Relatives tried to help us. They couldn't. They needed Mum to be strong to strengthen them.

We missed school. We were sick. No longer dressed neatly. Had no food. We were reported to the government as neglected children. An inspector came. She said she knew a white married couple in Sydney who would adopt or foster me. I was eight years old. My mother and our extended family didn't fight to keep me. No one talked about our problem. Except the welfare worker, who seemed to know best.

She was friendly and smiled and held my hand as we walked along the platform to the train for Sydney. My family and I hadn't said goodbye properly.

The house at Ashfield was bigger than our house. It was built of bricks with white wooden doors and white window shutters. Its roof was red. The garden had bright green lawns with borders of coloured flowers. A child's swing hung from a wooden frame.

There were no pepper trees. No trees at all, no vegetable garden. At our house in the country we had vegetables growing and fruit trees. Dad had made an irrigation system using water from the well.

The Thompsons, my foster-parents, had two older children in high school. It wasn't like having Willie laughing and squealing. I would have to be polite and quiet. A good girl. And shy. I knew my shyness always came back in difficult times.

I went to the public school. Nuns or teachers, I didn't mind. Things had to be different now. The happy time had gone. I didn't know how long I'd be able to remember Willie and Mum and Grandma Jane. I was beginning to forget my dad. I knew I still loved him.

In primary school I began to swim really well. My foster-mother took me to swimming pools for coaching and competition swimming. We became good friends. She told me to call her Nan, her name was Nanette. I was small for my age, she liked that. She said she'd had a brown Baby Betty doll when she was a little girl.

Primary school ended. High school began. Examinations were passed and always swimming with some prizes for first or second. And reading was my favourite pastime, relaxation and escape. I became fond of authors, they were my secret friends. Sometimes I'd dream about writing, perhaps poems or short stories to begin.

One more year of high school to go. I wouldn't be going to university. At least not at this time.

My foster-father's attitude towards me changed. When we were alone he'd look at me and whisper, 'You don't know how beautiful you've become.' 'You aren't my daughter. We don't have to pretend you are my daughter.' 'You call me Poppa. We've no blood relationship.' 'We can be more affectionate. It can be our secret.' 'You can't imagine how beautiful it can be.' What could I say?

My foster-mother must have sensed something was different. She seemed suspicious. That trust between us, even stronger than love, was weakening. Becoming sour and bitter. Nan and Poppa said angry things to each other. Their fights saddened me.

After their two children moved away from home, my swimming competitions had made me Nan's little girl. Suddenly I knew the meaning of the word conflict. If I told Nan what her husband whispered to me, I'd be disloyal. If

I said nothing and let the situation go on, I'd be weak, worthless.

What if I told Poppa to 'get real', that'd be the best. Did I have the courage? My shyness gets stronger and makes me weaker. I'm ashamed.

Again I thought about Poppa. He could have raped me. He didn't. He was talking to me, giving me a choice. I could handle this in a mature way. I thought how the older women talked at Grandma Jane's. It's strange how information long hidden in my brain came back when I needed it.

It is said that black people are cunning. Discrimination may have compelled them to resort to cunning. It's the weapon of the weak and oppressed against the strength of others. I can't say that discrimination has been my experience, except in this sexual harassment by my foster-father. And this could have happened to a white foster-daughter.

I believe the individual always has a choice. The only power another person has over us is the power we give him.

I thought, I'm too immature for my age. I'll continue at school and I'll get a part-time job. Work a few hours at weekends. And I need a boyfriend. A friendship. A boy I could talk to about almost everything. I don't want a sexual relationship, of course, I'm a schoolgirl. This plan would give my foster-parents the message that I'm becoming mature and more independent.

I remembered my favourite poem written by Kath Walker. I made a copy.

Away with bitterness, my own dark people,
Come stand with me, look forward, not back,
For a new time has come for us.
Now we must change my people. For so long
Time for us stood still; now we know
Life is change, life is progress,

Life is learning things, life is onward.
White men had to learn civilised ways,
Now is our turn.
Away with bitterness and the bitter past;
Let us try to understand the white man's ways
And accept them as they accept us;
Let us judge white people by the best of their race.

I went into the living room to tell my foster-father I was going to McDonald's to ask for part-time work. He said that was a good idea. I told him I'd make a copy of my favourite poem for him.

'Poppa, you and Nan are the two best people in the white race,' I told him.

'Thank you my dear,' he said. 'Nanette will be in shortly, we'll read the poem.'

As I left the house I told myself: I'm becoming more mature. And about time.

McDonald's gave me part-time work on Saturday evenings. I met Ronnie, a white Australian boy. After we finished our shift we drank a can of beer with the staff. At first I didn't like the taste. I discovered beer made my shyness disappear. A miracle. I could laugh and feel free. Be friendly and talk easily.

Soon Ronnie and I began to drink more beer, even to pass out. Sometimes we'd become aggressive and angry and get into fights. I was doing the thing I thought I'd never do. I was drinking like my mother. How could this happen?

One Saturday night we got into a fight at a pub. It was so bad the police came to break it up. A policeman arrested Ronnie. I kicked the policeman. He took me in as well. I was sixteen, Ronnie was seventeen.

At the police station they put us on two benches to sleep it off. Early Sunday morning they took our histories. The policeman I'd kicked was going off duty at six o'clock, he called to Ronnie:

'Romeo, take Juliet to the Drug and Alcohol Clinic, at Charles Street, to be admitted. Then go across to Western Suburbs Clinic and admit yourself. Both do a rehabilitation course, otherwise you'll become crims. I'm giving you a chance for a better life.'

That's how I came to be at group therapy with eight young women that Monday morning. I sat looking at the floor and wiped my sweaty palms down the sides of my jeans. I wasn't in good shape.

Each person in the circle had to say her name and why she was there. I said: 'I'm Julie and I'm an alcoholic. I kicked a cop because he arrested my boyfriend Ronnie. So he arrested me as well.'

No one laughed. We were a sick and sad lot that morning.

The counsellor was talking. Through a fog, I heard, 'You can learn to talk to each other in the group this first week. After three weeks you'll be going to live on the farm. Friday night before you leave here, there'll be an AA and NA meeting of about fifty people.

'You'll take responsibility for yourself. Walk out to the front, face the group, tell them who you are, how you got here, and where you're going. That's enough for now. When you're able to listen we'll talk again. In the meantime think, who took her first drink or drug because she was too shy to cope?'

She gave a small Bible, a notebook and a pen to each of us. 'You'll come to enjoy reading the Bible. The notebook is to write your autobiography. In rehabilitation people become writers and poets,' she said.

I settled in well. I imagined living in a college would be like this. Up early, prayers, physical exercises, breakfast, make beds. We helped with cooking, laundry and cleaning. After lunch we had to sleep for an hour. Time was set aside for reading, being quiet and group therapy.

We looked after the sick people, those hanging out for heroin, or hung over from alcohol. If a recovering addict was having a hard time drying out, two of us would stay with her. We needed each other.

After two weeks on the program a message came from Ronnie. A clinic supervisor phoned to say he'd like to visit me. Our director said no. She believed the addictive person must recover alone, away from family and old friends. I understood. It made me happy to hear that Ronnie remembered me.

I'd made him my whole family; that was too much love and responsibility for a seventeen-year-old sick boy. We would see each other again, but not yet.

I began to talk in groups. I'd say, 'I can relate to that.' We speak in our own special jargon in recovery groups. It's easier, more detached than trying to explain how we really feel. We are shy and sensitive. Usually we don't feel comfortable to blend in. We feel above the others or below them, never equal.

In group therapy we were told: Think back. You are two years old. You are downtown shopping with your mother. She meets two friends, they are happy to see each other. Then they speak to you. You hide your face in your mother's skirts. You won't speak. You've stopped their fun. Your mother says, 'She's shy,' you enjoy your power. You may kick and scream.

You may hold on to this childish behaviour throughout your life. Think about that. Could you find a better social skill? Perhaps help the people you meet to feel confident and happy. That's a better payoff.

That two-year-old child is still deep within all of us. Treat her gently. At this time when you're growing and changing, talk to her. At night when you're in bed, cross your arms over your chest and say to her, 'I'm becoming mature, I'll look after you. You don't have to feel timid or hurt.'

I phoned my foster-parents to ask whether they'd come to visit me on Wednesday evening of the third week. They

came. I told them I was sorry. They said they knew. Poppa
said, 'Remember your favourite poem,

Look forward not back ...
Life is learning things, life is onward ...
Away with bitterness and the bitter past.'

They told me to take time to get well. Then I'd know
how to plan my life. We'd been together for eight years
and we loved each other. Nan gave me a small wooden
crucifix with a figure of Jesus on the Cross.

'I remember you went to the nuns' school in the country. This might comfort you,' Nan said.

We cried and hugged and said goodbye.

At the AA meeting, when the time came, I walked to
the front and looked at the people. Not through my eye-
lashes but with my chin up I looked into their eyes. I told
them I was Julie, an alcoholic. I'd seen what alcohol had
done to my mother. With the power of God I was building
my life.

They clapped. Someone said, 'You'll do it, Julie.'

During that three weeks a counsellor worked with me
on my case history. It was good to remember the story of
my life.

I was a country girl and life on the farm appealed to
me. After three months I'd gained a little weight, become
clear-headed and confident. I was working with the chickens when an unexpected event occurred. Ronnie came to
the farm to visit me. He was happy. Free from alcohol for
more than three months.

'Nothing can stop us now,' he said.

I signed myself out from the farm program. And left
with him to go to Sydney.

Ronnie and I had changed in different ways. I didn't
want a life of drugs and alcohol. I wanted to learn new
ways of living and achieving my goals. I liked him, he was
my good friend.

Ronnie was so excited about being together that he

drank beer. He denied he had a problem and wasn't ready to give up using drugs. He was my sick friend.

I didn't drink or use drugs. After two days of wandering around, I phoned the farm from Sydney to ask if I could be admitted to continue my program. I was sorry I'd walked away. They said I could come back in twenty-eight days if I remained straight and sober. I thanked them. They suggested I should phone my foster-parents.

Nan and Poppa took me in again. Nan said I could go swimming every day. And I insisted I'd clean her windows. Funny I thought of that. I remembered that Mum and my dad, Henry Van Gough, often cleaned windows together. Out west we vacuumed our floors every day in the dusty season. My dad said the Dutch were hooked on house cleaning.

Nan's friend owned a plant shop at Ashfield and offered me a few hours' work. I said I didn't need any money, I'd like plants for Poppa's garden. The time passed quickly. I read and rested and when the twenty-eighth day came Nan and Poppa drove me to the farm.

Without further drama, I completed my rehabilitation in the usual nine months. At the farm they had a retired teacher come to tutor us. With his guidance I was able to complete my Higher School Certificate before leaving the farm.

One sunny Sunday afternoon early in April I walked along Charles Street. I was hoping to meet my counsellor coming to work at the Centre. We met and hugged each other. A happy moment. We sat on a wooden bench while I told her I'd been granted a scholarship to study welfare work. We both knew I was planning to help others to find what I had found.

I told her I was going to the far west to find my mother and Willie. I'd stay a week or two. I wasn't strong enough yet to spend a long time with them. When I'd finished my studies I'd see them again.

'Go gently,' she said, and walked towards the Centre to begin her day's work.

After ten years away from my family I'll have become a foreigner. I'll try to adjust. I hope to spend time to learn from them and to share with them what I've learned. Kath Walker said two cultures can blend, taking the best from each other.

I have a dream for my people. Throughout this country Aboriginal people can learn to work together. I learned at the recovery centre and at the farm, every person can become useful and efficient. Find joy in the work of his or her choice.

TAKING THE TALLY[1]

Susan Steggall

*Sister
Angela,
your time
& patience, your devotion,
have given me, simply, an
understanding, an insight,
chance glimpse
into that
tapestry
of living,
the time
of Assisi
- Clare -*

'How can women's lives be known when men write all the books?' asked Christine de Pisan, at the beginning of the fifteenth century.[2]

If history is a checklist of heroic deeds produced by men, a narrative that systematically excludes women from its mainstream, allowing them merely walk-on parts as helper, confidant or muse, how can women's achievements be recognised?

Language is fundamental to the social production of meaning; naming is all important. And if the masculine name stands for all, confining women to Madonna-Magdalena, where is there space for Ecclesia, Sapientia or Ende-Depintrix?[3] Feminist scholarship is now restoring their heritage and establishing links between women from different periods, places and persuasions. There are many stories to tell, many intellectual and aesthetic achievements to relate, many lives to be relived in prose, poetry and drama.

Mine is not an attempt to complete a life, tidy the lived spaces, round off corners and edges. Such a story would need an ending and the subject is very much alive. It is rather a glimpse into the life of a woman whose personal choices have not been easy; they would not suit everyone in contemporary Australia. It is in fact, two biographies: a paragraph in the narrative of women's scholarly and creative agency, in a tradition which stretches unbroken though frequently rendered invisible, from the thirteenth-century Italian Saint Clare of Assisi to the twentieth-century Australian Sister Angela of the St Clare monastery. It is because of two points in common — a passion for sculpture and a childhood geographical space — that I seized the chance to catch the momentum of an artist, of a sculptor who became a nun.

It would be impossible to complete the picture, to 'take the tally' of this life in contemporary Australia, without first a brief look at that of her mediaeval mentor. There are parallels in the lives of St Clare and Sister Angela — childhood freedom to explore the world, conventional yet eclectic education (Clare learned Latin and consequently had what Foucault calls the privileges of knowledge with access to the contemporary — priestly — language of control; Wendy was introduced to a sculptor's tools of trade at an early age by her surgeon father); equally strong-willed and not afraid to take risks or make difficult choices in their private lives. One could continue to seek and find many equivalencies, imagined or otherwise, in coincidences of life-marking events but this would begin to cross that interface between fiction and fancy, and 'a life' is the subject after all.

'Official' versions of the life and work of St Clare, such

as can be found, differ little in the bare facts — the bones —
to that recounted by Sister Angela. It is in the fleshing-out
of details where the telling diverges. Very briefly, Clare was
born in 1194 in Assisi into a noble Italian family. At the age
of eighteen she ran away from home to join Francis and his
order and become a nun. The Order of St Clare was mod-
elled as closely as possible upon that of the Franciscan
brothers, except that it was an enclosed order and the sisters might not leave the precincts of their convent. Clare
was adventurous and had wanted to do as the brothers did,
to travel and carry out missionary work. Nevertheless, so
history tells us, she remained within her convent walls,
governed for forty years and was canonised four years
after her death in 1253. She was well known in her lifetime,
advised and influenced the noble and powerful, including
popes and kings. She also corresponded with influential
women such as Agnes of Prague and Elizabeth, princess of
Hungary. 'She was a woman who would have found herself understood by Elizabeth Fry and Florence Nightingale,
but she was born before her time, in an era in which the
choice was between marriage or enclosure.' [4]

We do not know if Clare was an artist, yet if gardening
be an art, perhaps she was. It is recorded that she spent
much time in her small terrace garden, surrounded by
flowers; in the painting, 'St Clare and St Elizabeth', by
Filippo Memmi in Assisi,[5] she is shown with a lily in her
right hand, barefoot and dressed in simple clothes. What
is certain is that Clare chose the life of a nun rather than
submitting to society's mandatory rite of marriage. From
its origins in the sixth century, female monasticism had
maintained a tradition of theological and philosophical
scholarship, so the convent made it possible for women to
create and write. One could argue that as scholars, these
nuns contravened the 'natural' law of maternity and from
the tenth or eleventh centuries increasing restrictions
against ecclesiastical women included cloistering and the

imposition of confining, enshrouding clothing as forms of social control. Although churchmen who wrote about female sisters and saints tended to minimise their education and scholarship and emphasise their inspiration, mysticism and unwavering devotion to a (masculine) god, a tradition of educated and skilled women in religious orders persisted, with those who have remained in the history books usually seen as exceptions. But Clare was not an exception; there were many powerful, intelligent women, even among her own family, four of whom (mother, aunt and two sisters) joined the order.

The subject of my story became an artist almost by default, but a nun by determination. It is quite evident that from an early age the two most important factors in her life were already present — her energy and fascination with movement, and a need for the stillness of contemplation, a simplification of life to essentials. She had always wanted to capture the 'spiralling thing'[6] in the movement of living creatures and to reach back to the 'bare bones' of their existence. To begin with *to capture and to reach*, is perhaps plunging into the mainstream; to trace the origins one must return to the source.

Wendy Solling was born in 1926, one hundred years after the first inn and store were opened in the fledgling settlement of Wallis Plains, now the Hunter Valley town of Maitland. As early as the 1830s it was an important frontier centre of dusty streets crammed with bullock wagons carrying pioneer settler families and provisions as far north as the Queensland border would later be. They arrived by ship; sea and river being preferable to the risk of attack by bushrangers on the arduous overland route via the sandstone gorges of the Hawkesbury. The straggling village quickly grew into a prosperous rural community with the establishment of timber mills, farms, dairies, cattle and horse studs on the rich alluvial plains of the Hunter. For better or worse, Maitland's history has always

been linked to the river, although frequent and often violent floods have caused much damage to life and property.

The Solling family lived at the northern end of High
Street, a main thoroughfare too narrow for modern traffic,
at the angle where the former bullock track turns to cross
rich farmland and lead up to the Campbell's Hill sale-
yards; regular weekly stock sales were important events,
commercially and socially, for outlying farming families.
From East Maitland and the site of the first tollgate over
Wallis Creek, the road winds through the main town, past
hitching posts, relics of the days of horse-drawn vehicles,
and past its numerous corner pubs that, though refur-
bished and camouflaged, are still reminders of the town's
rough-and-ready past.

Here Wendy spent her childhood, growing up with the
sounds and smells of the horses and sulkies of the
Depression years, the drovers and their cattle. Her world
oscillated between the smithy and the surgery. At the forge,
she would sit for hours, more at home in the blacksmith's
workshop than a cubby house, more at ease with hammer
and chisel than conventional toys. She says with a laugh, 'I
was a bit of a menace as a kid — hammers and nails were
my medium — not dolls. Nobody except the family knew
that I was so interested in sculpture, at that time.'

And then there was her love of horses. Appropriately,
stone-chisels, her first set of carving tools, were made from
the steel of the farrier's old files.

She remembers looking down from her balcony on to
the passing parade, relishing the clipping pace of the
horses' hooves, the crack of the stockmen's whips as they
flickered in the fraction of space above the animals' backs,
the music of Newton's forge, the noise and bustle of
horse, man and steer. It was a splendid scene of colour,
sound, smell and above all movement, which left lasting
impressions on an energetic yet sensitive child, influences
that re-emerged later in her sculpture.

School holidays were spent in the company of her two brothers as 'the filling in the middle', roaming the grassy plains of her father's home country of Moree or the rolling pastures of the Hunter Valley where she remembers helping drove cattle from outlying districts to the town, frosty early mornings droving out Aberglasslyn way, getting the cattle in with old Blue Lewis, shivering with cold and excitement, the mystery and poetry of sunrise.

Due to recurrent bronchitis, as she tells it, 'I grew too quickly,' she was sent to boarding school in Moss Vale where it was hoped the bracing air of the Southern Tablelands would improve her health. There she quickly regained her strength and health and began to rebel against the conventions and restrictions of a girl's education. The company of father and brothers, drovers and blacksmith, had been a very masculine world, of considerable freedom and adventure.

At school she requested drawing classes, but found the static still-life arrangements and the emphasis on perspective and shading little to her liking. She became dissatisfied and restless with the endless, repetitive exercises imposed on her by a teacher who could not or would not see that she longed to draw a tree, to catch its form, its movement, to catch action — a girl riding a bike, or a horse galloping: 'the actual mobility of what this was'. So she abandoned the art lessons and began to carve straight into whatever material was available — fence post, tennis-court post or wooden ruler.

Perhaps because of her father's influence and her early awareness of a need to find the essence of things, she had always been interested in healing work and she seriously considered studying medicine. However she was influenced by the prevailing attitude that professional careers were wasted on girls and instead enrolled at East Sydney Technical College under the tutelage of sculptor Lyndon Dadswell in 1945, in the first intake after World War II.

Many of the male students had come to art school straight from the army so that the optimism and energy of those immediate post-war years made Sydney an exciting and dynamic place.

In 1947, like so many ambitious young Australians, Solling made the pilgrimage to London. Although she was rather lonely, she thoroughly enjoyed the world of the Tate Gallery, Bond Street and all the latest exhibitions and paintings. She called it a 'very vital time'; not surprising since she herself imbues all with infectious enthusiasm and energy. Initially she followed the traditional path for newly arrived 'colonial' artists and studied at the Slade, but found it had not much to offer after her thorough and rigorously technical Australian art education, so left to take up a studio in Chelsea where many of her wire sculptures were completed.

Yet contemplation and artistic creation had always been intertwining threads running through her life. If contemplation means shedding the inessentials and seeking the unadorned shape of existence, 'the bare bones of what Clare is about', her decision to abandon for a time the sculptor's conventional materials of wood, plaster and stone and to eliminate colour and embellishment from her work was a logical progression in harmony with her need to strip unnecessary artifice from daily existence. She began making figures simply in armature wire, 'to let the wire speak for itself', creating three-dimensional black-and-white drawings; using the filament's own sinuous curves to create movement and its cast shadows for shading as 'we humans also make our own shading'.

It was not so much homesickness as an expatriate's longing for the spaciousness of the Australian plains with a touch of nostalgia for the magic of her childhood droving days — the cuppa over the fence, the swearing and cursing at the stockyards, the 'mystery and the poetry' in the frosty light of early morning musters — that led to the use of such icons of national identity as the bullocky, drover and shearer, and titles for her works such as 'Breaking In', 'The Drover and Dog', and 'The Bullocky and His Whip'. She remembers those school holidays 'up Moree way' where in the heat and glaring, brilliant dryness, everything, even clothing, is stripped to a bare minimum. The grasslands with their interminable wire fences are dry, parched expanses, littered with the sun-dried bones of animals. Truly, 'a land that could dry out the body and spirit'.[7]

Wendy Solling shares with the poet Judith Wright not only the imagery of these very male Australian heroes but the same insistence on bone, bare and bleached. In the wire sculptures there is not the bravado of much masculine representation; the drover is not presented as a man in action, but in a moment of rest, the horse's head hanging tiredly down — 'the bone whisper[ing] in the hide'.[8] The insubstantiality of the wire frame alludes to the passing of an era, evoking a sense of the vulnerability and isolation of human existence. In Wright's verse too, the bullocky is rendered vulnerable by obsolescence, when 'Grass is across the wagon-tracks, and plough strikes bone beneath the grass',[9] with farms and vineyards now covering the hillsides. The ghosts of dead teams and the fine-drawn shadows of wire sculptures become ghostly mementoes, in marked contrast to the swirling, dusty action in much masculine art and poetry that invariably stands for our national identity.

Again the drover, at one with his horse and constantly on the move, epitomises the poet's spiritual journey into the country of the self and this artist's own search for creative and spiritual identity. These wire sculptures indicate, in retrospect, her later decisions and commitments. The sense of isolation in Solling's lanky, spare frames, each claiming its solitary space, is also reminiscent of Giacometti's elongated, emaciated figures, not only for their etiolated form but also for that impression of distancing from the everyday world.

Many of her early works in wood also retain that essence of leanness: for example, 'Hands of Service' is shaped as a tall, tragic figure with worn gnarled hands, carved from an old tennis-court post found in an English garden. Solling says, 'I got the idea for this figure when sitting on the steps of Tours cathedral in France, watching an ageing Fransciscan monk walk slowly up a hill.'

Solling came back to Australia in 1952 with a solo exhibition in September at the David Jones art gallery. Then followed her freelance period, a successful though somewhat financially precarious existence. She enjoyed its freedom, '...on the smell of an oil rag — something in the bank one week, nothing the next but never absolutely broke, it was a good way to live'.

She obtained many commissions for portrait busts, including that of singer Rosina Raisbeck, also from Maitland, and Hans Christian Andersen, commissioned by Sydney's Danish community in 1955. This work was removed from its plinth in Phillip Park near St Mary's cathedral under mysterious circumstances; she laughs now about the theft of a bust constructed of fibreglass with merely a bronze skin. She was also one of only two women sculptors chosen to participate in the group exhibition held by the Society of Sculptors and Associates at the David Jones art gallery in 1955, in which the works she exhibited were not only in wire but of wood and metal, abstracted to an essence, yet by their titles, 'Flood Wrack' and 'Face of the Land', linked to that country of her childhood.

Although she was now developing a successful career as a sculptor, not an easy goal for a woman in the 1950s in Australia — or anywhere for that matter — a need for contemplation and a growing religious faith were gradually leading her more firmly towards her decision to become a nun, even though, as she put it, her family was 'low church Anglican' and she knew nothing about nuns or monks, religious orders or their traditions.

Her first contact with what she was seeking came in 1955 when she was creating a sculpture for the chapel garden at the Morpeth theological college and later met a Franciscan friar out from England at a retreat in Sydney. She found that it was not what he said, but was rather a special kind of love that came through him, and she determined to find out more about it. The turning point came while lecturing on her work at Women's College, Sydney University; she had one of the first of several 'out-of-body' experiences, seemingly a dialogue between her creative and spiritual selves, in conflict at that moment. She had the impression that while she was talking, there was another self sitting out with the students, saying, 'You don't believe a word you're saying.'

She replied to this other, 'Look here, you give me a gift of sculpture; that's what I'm meant to be doing, not going off and being a crazy nun.'

Then Wendy realised she must become a nun, but that she must also continue her work as an artist, a paradox that was to test her for many years.

Because of this inescapable attraction to devotion through contemplation, Solling felt she had to find out about St Clare. She decided to go back to England, even though it meant renouncing the conventional path for a woman and artist — a family and a publicly visible career — for a very different life in a devotional sisterhood with a difficult inner creative journey to negotiate. She returned to the United Kingdom in 1956, passed her test of vocation and entered an enclosed, contemplative order, remaining there until 1975.

And so Wendy Solling became Sister Angela ...

Those years were not always easy; enclosure and vows of silence must have been hard for a girl brought up in the freedom and open space of the Australian countryside. As a novice sister she continued to sculpt, carving large pieces in white sandstone, taking them off their plinths and outside into open spaces, 'as meditation things, you see', calling every piece a prayer. Solling's earlier secular works had been very successful, finding their way into many public and private collections. Since taking orders her work has changed, dramatic yet peaceful with the power of contemplation, the angular planes of face and body providing the colour and shading. Their carved forms have acquired volume, become anchored to the sand in which she placed them; her own energy was now contained, her sculptures no longer free to move.

There was a time after the novice years when Sister Angela was occupied with administrative concerns with little time for sculpture, and she knew she had been given creativity as a balance to her faith. Once again she experienced that curious sensation of two selves in dialogue although this time a more powerful element seemed to be present. The experience is best described in her own words.

About six years down the track, I was doing a big sculpture, it was eight feet tall, a Resurrection Christ leaping off a cross, seventy feet up in the air, in a modern church. The scaffolding had to come down on a certain date and the sculpture had to be on the wall by then.

It was exhausting work, and I was frozen, in an unfinished shed with the water and snow seeping in, and God said, 'What do you think you're doing?'

And I said (angrily), 'Trying to carve this image of you in this wood!'

The reply came back, 'That's not what's happening. I am carving my image in you as you are doing it.'

Now this is a big thing, I made a mistake. I didn't hear that little word 'as'. What was said to me was,

'While you are doing that carving, I am doing my work in you as you do the carving'.

As you do the carving. I forgot that last bit. So that when I had to cut my time down for sculpture — it dropped out almost — [it] was a terrible mistake. Because it was given to me for balance.

Here, tradition links the twentieth century to earlier times. Sister Angela belongs to that heritage of artist nuns, reaching back to the convent of Chelles in Carolingian times, where Gisela directed the production of illuminated manuscripts by women scribes.[10] Perhaps best known is the eleventh-century Hildegard of Bingen, a visionary, an artist and a great contemplative nun, and like Clare, a politically active woman who corresponded with kings and queens, emperors and empresses.[11]

After eighteen years, Sister Angela returned to Australia to establish the St Clare monastery in Stroud, New South Wales. She has been the energy and guiding force behind the creation of a series of buildings linked by covered wooden walkways, whose design and construction reflect a sculptor's eye for colour, line and material. The sun-fired earth brick *is* the landscape, the sculpted forms *are* the trees.

Sister Angela laughs as she recalls the trials and errors of building. They built the brothers' house first, to learn by early mistakes, and adapted their technique as they went along. Construction began in 1977 and was completed eighteen months later, with the dedication of the monastery taking place in 1980. It was a remarkable feat for a small group of nuns and the many friends and acquaintances who willingly trampled the wet earth for the hand-made bricks. It consists of dining-room, sisters' residences and visitors' quarters. Not surprisingly, there is a large and well equipped sculpture workshop where Sister Angela works on her commissions; she also works with the others, making small wooden pieces (crosses and carvings) to sell in the community shop. The community is one giant earth sculpture, an inhabited work of art, a living tribute to the singular vision of a woman of formidable creative talents and religious faith.

The chapel is perhaps the most ambitious building. There is the same external anonymity but inside there is simplicity with a special luminosity. The rammed-earth floor, plain wooden furniture and deceptively simple sculptures create an atmosphere at once welcoming and reverential. The sunlight filters through stained glass windows designed by a sister as paintings. They were translated into glass by an eighty-year-old master craftsman in Paris. Sister Angela indicates her sculpture, again a Resurrection Christ, created as something that would truly catch the eye, act as a focus for one's thoughts. The figure has no facial features, no bodily form. It's 'just an explosion of energy, that upward surge.' And the cross: 'It's just a piece of wood from the hills, but again, exploding with energy.'

I visited the monastery recently, driving north on the freeway to Hexham then taking a series of ever-narrowing roads lined with giant eucalypts, the air pervaded by the aromatic tang of freshly cut timber, a reminder that logging is still an important local industry. Sadly the once-abundant native cedar is no more, although Sister Angela has managed to retrieve several gnarled and knotted old stumps to transform in her singular fashion. I approached the cluster of low, dun-coloured buildings with some diffidence, not at all sure how someone many years away from any contact with formal religious observance should behave, should address someone of such strong conviction. I was immediately put at ease by the openness of the place, its air of welcome and the dynamic presence of Sister Angela herself, a tall spare figure dressed in a simple cotton dress and bareheaded, without the confining robes and wimple of Clare's century. It was an interview conducted in snatches, the constant demands on her time and her enthusiasm for the place itself preventing her from remaining immobile for long.

She told me that they had had to build because there was literally nowhere to live. For the first few years all her time and energy went into building the monastery, with little time for sculpture. When the community's existence was assured, she felt spent, denuded of energy — physically and emotionally — and 'went bush' for six months, living as a hermit. Naturally, for someone for whom contemplation is a necessary aspect of life, she took with her a puzzling question: What do Aborigines mean when they say that 'the earth speaks at last light and at first light'?

She spent much time searching, almost despairing of an answer. Then the idea came to her that she wasn't asking the right question. In her own words, she had been concentrating on what was being said, instead of who was speaking. She began to understand, as Aboriginal peoples have always done, that it was Mother Earth who was speaking; Mother Earth from whom all things come. This insight, the solution to her problem, had come as always, in prayer and contemplation. Her own energy and creativity were renewed: 'This whole concept exploding in me so that when I came out, I came out a feminist, didn't I?'

Early in 1994 Sister Angela spent four months in the United States on an episcopal fellowship, embarking on a new career as a feminist theologian. She returned more firmly than ever committed to her chosen life's path with St Clare's example ever before her; and a new determination to seek out, define and support women's purpose and place in the contemporary world. Sister Angela has spent many years studying Clare's remarkable life and considers her to have been one of the earliest feminists.

Clare's intelligence and individuality were inevitably subsumed under Francis's reputation so that by the twentieth century, she is virtually known to the world only through his deeds, her name known only through his. In historical novels that cast a gloss of sanctity over the lives of Clare and Francis, concealing and smoothing the roughs of human frailty and doubt, Clare is always woman-as-saint, obedient to her heavenly father and to her earthly master, Francis, seeking salvation and comfort through prayer, heroic self-denial, poverty and abstemious living.

She is mother superior, the maternal instinct never allowed to disappear: 'Though she held the nuns to their strict discipline she had for them the same tenderness that Francis had for the brothers ... and all her maternity was poured out upon them.'[12]

The rediscovery of Clare's Rule is perhaps one of the great theological detective stories of the twentieth century. Books make no mention of it, only that Clare and the nuns tried with much pain and difficulty to adhere to the almost impossible conditions laid down by Francis. Sister Angela, however, believes otherwise. Clare was the first woman to write a Rule. She spoke and wrote Latin, but her Rule contained such key ideas that, although the pope signed it, the canon lawyers and the brothers wanted it destroyed. And so Clare's Rule disappeared, remaining hidden for more than five centuries, sewn into an old habit of Clare's and placed in a relic box, 'where no man would think of looking!' It was recognised quite recently by an archivist and is now in the church of Chiara in Assisi for all to see. Perhaps somewhat controversially, Sister Angela maintains that Clare was not confined by enclosure, that she created a sanctuary for prayer, not a prison, and included riders to the Rule that opened up many eventualities where enclosure should not be enforced. 'She just got around all the obstacles. Clare's last sentence was [I think] an exhortation to women not to give up.'

An important aspect of Sister Angela's faith is the need to share her knowledge and to tell women, especially those who are confined and not free to choose their own way, what Clare was saying and fighting for. Sister Angela considers it important to make public the lives of such women and so is writing a book about Clare, to get all the information on record, before exploring other dramatised ways of telling.

Men, she feels, are often frightened by the unfamiliarity, perhaps of women taking the ordering of the world into their own hands and she regrets that though there are men who support and encourage the liberation of women in both the physical and intellectual sense, they are sadly but few. She feels also, that when men retire, they give up. But as she says, 'I'm an old-age pensioner and I'm starting something new!'

She wants to break out of the confines of a tradition that has grown increasingly restrictive over the centuries. She is resolute in her conviction that it is not Clare's tradition to stay enclosed in fear, superstition and prejudice. Clare's 'tradition' is to break free of confining obstacles. Sister Angela is determined to stay in the church, to emulate not only Clare who stuck to it and fought the church from inside, but all those who rebel against unjust systems. She feels she cannot criticise the church from the outside, 'You're priested, you're in there,' she says simply.

I leave with my newly bought holding-cross and feel comforted by its tag: the prosaic name, address and telephone number on one side and on the other a more spiritual exhortation to hold it firmly in the knowledge that someone is praying with and for you. While I do not share Sister Angela's religious conviction, I can only admire her commitment, energy and devotion to her faith and her art.

Here I close the tale, not at the ending, not with its final chapter; in fact, there will be many more chapters to write and challenges to follow. At the threshold of Sister Angela's new career, this story ends, or perhaps halts to take stock. Wendy Solling–Sister Angela is a woman living in three convergent traditions: firstly, as a nun in an illustrious company of devout women reaching back to the founding Franciscan orders of Assisi and beyond; secondly, as an artist in that long tradition of creative women, now being brought in from the Stygian obscurity to which masculine insecurity had relegated them; and thirdly, simply, to the sisterhood of Australian women who create and work imaginatively in a 'man's country' where the land itself often dominates and is dominated by the masculine.

Mother Earth, Saint Clare *and* Sister Angela.

1 'Taking the Tally' is the title of one of the artist's wire sculptures exhibited at the Galerie Apollinaire in London in 1951.

2 Chadwick, Whitney, *Women, Art and Society*, Thames and Hudson, UK, 1990, p. 30.

3 Depintrix was a painter; recently identified as the artist who illuminated the Beatus Apocalypse of Gerona in mediaeval Spain, Chadwick, *op. cit.*, p. 41.

4 Goudge, Elizabeth, *Saint Francis of Assisi*, UK, 1959.

5 Reproduced in *A Calendar of Saints*, by Vincent Cronin, London, 1963.

6 All quotes, unless otherwise stated, were recorded in a conversation with the artist in December 1993.

7 Smith, Bernard, Introduction to 'Hardship and Weird Melancholy', *Documents of Art & Taste*, Oxford University Press, Australia/UK, 1975.

8 Wright, Judith, 'Drought Year' in *Collected Poems*, A&R Modern Poets edition, Sydney, 1975, p. 85.

9 *Ibid.*, 'Bullocky', p. 17.

10 Chadwick, *op cit.*, p. 40.

11 In her study of Hildegard, Barbara Newman identified her as the first Christian thinker to deal seriously and positively with the idea of the feminine, shown as Eve, Mary and Ecclesia [Mother Church]. At the heart of her spiritual world are the images of Sapientia and Caritas, visionary and female forms of Holy Wisdom and Love Divine; Chadwick, *op. cit.*, p. 49.

12 Goudge, *op cit.*, p. 132.

THE PROLAPSE

Rae Luckie

I really like Stephen King's writing. Not that I did much reading in hospital. I couldn't concentrate. Trish, my eldest, had armed me with horror books but I only browsed through the *Women's Weekly, New Idea* and a couple of *Telegraph Mirrors*. The Sister brought the 'Tellies' around every morning. Trouble was that if you napped, the pink-uniformed cleaning duo whipped them away before eleven. Didn't like the room looking messy.

I was scared sick the couple of weeks before the operation. Half the time I couldn't sleep and the night before I went into hospital I played Tetris Max on the Apple Macintosh. All night. Tetris is supposed to be all the rage for women. It's not a 'shoot the baddies' game. You try and stack different-shaped coloured bricks into neat rows, and work your way up the levels.

The higher the faster
   Click the brick right
      Click the brick left
         Down
            and
               down
      Each brick link makes a click
            Coloured links make a clack
      A full row makes a CRASH
            New level cow moos

click clack crash moo swish swish click click
husky flutes beating drums trilling chimes
click crash moo beat beat beat dum de dum

I was still wondering if I had done the right thing. Made the decision, that is. The gynaecologist always left it up to me. 'You'll know when,' he said, and I suppose I did, even though it took fourteen years.

It's amazing what you'll put up with, but it just creeps up over time. The back pain. Excessive bleeding. I remember October 1991. I was organising my middle child Tracy's wedding and began bleeding. I was coping with a new job, travelling two days to work and three days to the University of Technology. All that plus study, lesson preparation and teaching. Tracy and Tony had an on-again, off-again romance for eight years. The phone rang.

Guess what?

What?

I'm pregnant.

PREGNANT PAUSE.

Can you organise the wedding before Christmas before I begin to show?

I'll call you back.

I have a little weep first.

Still bleeding at the wedding the week before Christmas, and on through the holidays at the beach at Hawks Nest. Visits to the GP — perhaps it was the hormone replacement therapy? Back to the specialist. Checks my history.

'How's the urine problem,' he asks. Of course we never talk about things like that do we? Apart from 'Continence Week' and then it's really incontinence we're talking about.

I turned forty in 1980. I remember I needed to put a neatly folded Kleenex into my breezeweight sensible full brief flesh-coloured Bonds (Made in Australia) Cottontails.

Just in case. Then at least two or three. What a relief when panty pads came on the scene! My incontinence began with the odd drop when I sneezed or coughed. If I was on a health kick and tried to jog, I made sure I stuck in a full-size pad. By the early 1990s I began wearing pads all the time. Oh yes, I did the pelvic floor exercises, but I'll admit it: I hate dieting and exercise and I like food and wine (but not Chateau Cardboard because you never remember how much you drink). Eventually I enjoyed a bottle to myself most nights, chardonnay because I often felt stressed and it helped the aches and pains. And I put on the weight. Although I didn't smoke — a good thing — I was fat, and the contraceptive pill wasn't considered a good idea. So I went into Jamieson private hospital for a tubal ligation. The heavy bleeding began and it was back in again a few times for a D & C. I could never understand why hormone replacement therapy was a good idea if the pill was a bad idea, but I've been on HRT ever since the hot flushes began. I read in Germaine Greer's book *The Change* that it's a bad idea, but I think maybe if I go off it now I'll crumble away to dust like an Egyptian mummy that has just been unwrapped. You've seen the movie, haven't you?

Which brings me to 'The Prolapse'. Whenever I think of it I remember Frankie Howard in *Up Pompeii* doing 'The Prologue'. English comedy, black and white. Now let's be frank — how would you like your insides beginning to fall through to the outside? The specialist tried to put it delicately.

'Do you feel anything poking outside your vagina at times?'

'Well,' I said, 'I don't go around feeling myself but I think sometimes maybe I notice something not quite right when I have a shower or wipe after going to the toilet.'

'Does it feel something like a nose?'

'I suppose so — I don't really know.'

'Is it a hard little nose or a soft little nose?'

I burst into tears.

'I don't know — how hard is a nose?'

'Well don't worry about it too much, but if it's more like a hard nose it's your cervix.'

A nose is a rose.

But I kept ignoring things. More bleeding. More leakage. More dragging back pains. New GP. She looked and said, 'That's a really significant prolapse you've got there — have you thought about getting something done about it?'

So she referred me back to the same specialist who first suggested the hysterectomy around the mid-1980s. It had to be my decision. I suppose it's because if anything goes wrong with the operation you can't say you were pressured into it. Specialists are worried about litigation.

To remove or not to remove? That is the question. The removal of my uterus. I haven't got any psychological hang-ups about it. At least, I don't think I have. I don't equate having a womb as being an essential part of my female identity. Being fat is. My parents had divorced when I was young and I lived with my mother's sister Madge and her husband in Orange. When I was little I had cute blue eyes and blonde hair. Then I got fat. I was the only fat kid I knew. I look around now and think I'd probably be hardly noticed in the McDonald's and KFC generation.

(Are you too fat too fat too fat? Take Ford Pills — or was it Dr Mackenzie's Menthoids?)

Inside my head I feel okay most of the time, but at other times my body becomes all-encompassing. Especially when I'm still waking up with the same odd pains in the night and the morning. The pains you can't explain.

I haven't got my top teeth either. Had them ripped out when I was in first year at high school. The worst part was waiting for six months for my gums to shrink so I could be fitted with an upper denture.

It all began when I used to pretend I had gone to the dentist and filled my teeth with chewing gum fillings to fool my aunt. I used to get presents for being such a brave girl going on my own. That's when I started taking Vincents APCs. I was eleven. My aunt took them at least four or five or more times a day. They used to be given away as prizes on radio quizzes and she was often the lucky winner. Large size twelve-pack boxes. 24 x 12 precious pink pain-killing powders in blue and yellow printed wrappers. I'd begin by taking one from each pack so she wouldn't notice. When she became a bit suspicious I'd steal money from my Uncle Bill's trouser pocket. He had a little coin purse in the fob and left the pipe-smoke-smelling thick tweed trousers hanging overnight behind the bathroom door. Two shilling pieces then the odd ten-shilling or pound note just to buy Codral for the toothache. Small blue-labelled brown bottles with a black lid which made a popping noise when it was eased off. Pull out the cotton wool protecting the white tablets and munch and crunch and poke the residue into gaping decaying holes to stop the throbbing pain.

Tracy, Tony and our two grandkids were here in July. Just before I went into hospital for the hysterectomy. Tracy was going through an old shoebox full of photos waiting patiently in the bottom of the wardrobe. She pulled out our sepia hand-tinted wedding photo. I had on a short white dress and veil and white shoes with high heels and pointy toes. We both looked so young and happy and I was slim and pretty. Prescribed Dexedrine had done the trick. Take just one maroon and black capsule first thing in the morning. Wait for the little rush of energy and get through the housework like a dervish. But then I used to get an anxious feeling in the afternoon and I often couldn't sleep at night.

I was introduced to corsets when I was eleven. My aunt used to give me her old ones, tough patterned pink cottoned boned seams with criss-cross laces. You started lacing from the bottom — catch the hooks and cross pull tight as you go right up to just under the bust then wind the lace once around your waist and tie in a bow at the front. Breathe out. The top of the corset often parted company with the short bra and I'd have a neat roll of pink flesh bulging out all around. I remember going to David Jones for a fitting for the first corset that wasn't a hand-me-down. The sales assistant ran her eyes down her nose and over my trembling sixteen-year-old obesity. 'Modom has a pendulum stomach.'

If you are wondering what a pendulum stomach is, borrow *Mrs Doubtfire* from your local video store. She wore a beautifully constructed padded beige stomach with matching rubber breasts underneath her carefully constructed wrinkled face. Peel off the fat-body suit and underneath Robin Williams was trim taut and terrific. But with a real pendulum as you get older, bacterium lurks under the folds waiting to turn into itching painful rashes. Worse in summer.

I remember under my wedding dress I wore a white all-in-one lacy strapless model with bones biting up under the breasts. I used to get savage red marks and then scabs where the bones ground in. Four clip-on suspenders embraced the stocking tops. I still wear a Playtex lycra all-in-one cross-your-heart body suit, size 20 D, but at weekends I like staying in my gown and slippers all day.

Incontinence finally gets to you when you can feel the pad filling even when you're not jogging, sneezing or coughing and you begin to wonder whether people around you can smell the odour. The ammonia smell of a baby's nappy. So you change pads every couple of hours. Then it gets worse. You get obsessive to ensure that you've always got a pad handy. Pads with wings. Supersize without wings at night. In bags, purses, make-up bags, in the car, in the drawers at work. I always have a spare in my bra. Just in case.

The final straw — being unable to control the dribble down the left leg between cleaning teeth at the basin and stepping towards the shower. The majority of women in nursing homes are supposed to be there because of incontinence so it can't just be happening to me, but nobody talks about it. My mother-in-law lost control of her mind but not her bladder. She died from a broken memory. What's worse?

So then it's back to the gynaecologist. Questions and recorded answers. Remove your lower garments. Lie down on the waterproof blue square. Cough. Don't feel embarrassed, cough harder. And you know his hands are getting wet. 'There's more than one problem,' he said, staring over his half specs.

'The prolapse, bleeding and incontinence aren't necessarily related,' he said, 'so we'll get some tests done for the incontinence.' I love the way doctors say 'we', don't you? 'They're not pleasant,' he said. He explained the prolapse was caused by the weakening and collapse of the pelvic floor muscles from a number of causes probably relating to childbirth (x 3), overweight, standing, and loss of oestrogen after menopause. 'Just think of your pelvic floor like a hammock which is holding everything up — uterus, bladder and bowel. After the uterus is removed, I'll stitch back the bladder and bowel and reconstruct the vagina. Your vagina will be as good as it was thirty years ago.' He drew a diagram.

A song began running around in my head. I imagined I was in a crazy Dennis Potter-like scene. A chorus line of blowzy middle-aged high-kicking women.

> *A one two three four*
>> *link your arms and tap-hop-shuffle*
>>> *and tap and kick and step and kick*
>>>> *and step and kick and step and kick*
> *a one two three four*
>> *and turn your heads to the left*
>>> *and turn your heads to the right*
>>>> *and smile and sing and tap hop shuffle*
> *and a one two three four all together now …*

Nothing could be finer
than to have a new vagina
in the mor–hor–hor–ning
Nothing could be neater
than the stitching when I greet yer
in the mor–hor–hor–ning

Well, it was nearing the end of semester and I had students facing the run up to final exams. I couldn't get an appointment out of class time with the urologist at the Castlereagh Radiography Centre, so I delayed for another month.

The Things They Do to 'Dear'(Part 1)

'Drink at least a litre of water two hours before the appointment and don't go to the toilet, dear.' Dear wonders if she'll disgrace herself in front of the dozens of patients waiting. One of the staff just goes around tidying dog-eared magazines. 'Would you like a cup of tea, dear?' She smiles. Dear says, 'No, thanks,' holds her knees together and tries to hold in the bulging hammock. Dear buries her head wondering what is going to happen when it's her turn.

Nurse smiles and directs Dear to a small room with an ordinary toilet and a contraption like an upturned megaphone. 'Put this on, take everything off below the waist then wee in there, dear,' she says, pointing to the megaphone. Dear puts on the blue disposable gown and notices the megaphone-like object has what looks like a microphone in it with a couple of leads disappearing under the door. Later Dear notices they're attached to a Macintosh powerbook computer. The specialist asks questions beginning with childhood illnesses. 'Do you leak when you have intercourse?' Dear blushes: 'Well, I don't know I — er — well I — er haven't — you know — er for a number of years.' The questions go on and on. Finally he asks Dear if she is widowed or divorced.

'Um — er I've been happily married for thirty-three

years,' Dear says. She hides her embarrassment by expressing interest in the Apple Macintosh's part in the procedure. She's told to lie on the narrow X-ray table and the Mac is behind her head. First an ultrasound. Dear tells about seeing her second grandchild on ultrasound. Watching the little mite bouncing and jiggling around.

'He's now six months old,' Dear says.

I went to his birth.

Broken Hill 17 January 1994
Tracy woke in the morning with some pains. Seven minutes apart. She and Tony walked around the corner to the hospital while Barry and I got breakfast for seventeen-month-old Raynor. It was going to be a long hot day in the town of red dust, artists and slagheaps. The midwife checked Tracy out and said she could go back home. Anxious, tense. Raynor had almost died at birth.

Trace had a big vomit around lunch time and had a couple of unusual pains which worried her, so she and Tony went back. Around 10 pm after Barry and I had settled Raynor for the night I went around to the maternity ward. Tracy wanted me to be there and I was really scared.

10.15 pm
Tony is lying on the labour ward floor reading John Grisham's *The Firm*. The birthing bed is in two main sections, upper and lower, and Tracy has control of the back section. It can be raised up or down and go back and forward. There are plenty of pillows. I can see a trolley with double shelves, the top one holding a perspex bassinette and hovering above an infra-red lamp ready for the baby. A few packages wrapped in forest green linen are on another trolley. Stainless steel. Cream walls. Grey floor. Two midwives bustle in and out of the ward. She's having long strong contractions. They think she will give birth soon so they're not going to give her a pethidine needle.

I sit in the corner and watch and wait. Everyday conversation between contractions weaves in and out of the tension in the air. Tony just keeps on reading. I wonder if he ought to be near her? She looks so alone. I'd like to go over but I don't want to be between them. The baby should be born before midnight, they think.

Midnight
Tracy still quiet. Not complaining. Silent suffering. It's been eleven hours of really strong contractions and she looks absolutely exhausted. I feel so helpless.

1 am
Both midwives seem just a little bit concerned. They've each had a try at rupturing the membranes because she's fully dilated. The contractions are exceptionally long and strong but still between five and eight minutes apart. Tracy's in obvious pain but not saying a word. They don't seem to think the baby is in distress. Tony walks over and rubs her neck.

I hear the baby's fluttering heartbeat through the monitor and watch the graph charting the contractions. You can tell when the babe is kicking. Green digits flash. Now it's 165 beats a minute, now 120, up, down, up, down. I wonder if it should be doing that? Please please let everything be all right.

The doctor phones and says he will leave it up to the midwives. The local doctors won't deliver babies at Broken Hill hospital so it's a visiting locum from Wollongong.

Tony is still reading the same page of the book. Tracy is sitting like a Buddha, sometimes stroking her tummy and talking to the baby. I'm silently panicking when they lose the heartbeat momentarily.

2 am
The night is dragging on. Tony goes out for a smoke. I go

over and stroke Tracy's forehead and hold her hand. 'Leave me alone,' she says and grits her teeth and I go back to my corner and hold the tears back. Why did I come? 'Would you like me to go?' I ask. 'No, I want you to stay,' she says.

3 am

Tracy starts to vomit. At the same time lightly stained mucus is spilling from her vagina on to a large blue plastic-backed pad underneath. Tracy begins to use the gas. The midwife says she's sorry they didn't give her the pethidine. Tracy still doesn't complain and vomits again. Tony is rubbing her back. They give her a heat pad and it seems to help. 'Are you sure you don't feel like pushing?' they ask Tracy. 'No.' she says. She continues to retch but there's nothing to bring up.

4.45 am

'I want to get on my hands and knees,' Tracy says.

   'Do you want to push?'

   'No, I just might feel better on my hands and knees.'

   They help her to turn over and she is kneeling on the lower half of the bed, head on the top half. I wonder how long this can go on. But the midwives begin moving briskly and putting on forest green gowns and gloves. Still the long distance between hard contractions. I begin to think there must be something wrong.

   She begins a contraction and muffles a moan. I'm looking at her buttocks. I have a front row seat. I didn't expect it. I thought I'd be somewhere beside her but I'm sitting in the corner opposite her splayed-apart legs. There's thick, heavily bloodstained mucus dripping and I almost panic as I see faeces appear above and suddenly below it there's a rather slimy greenish-looking bulge. One midwife quickly wipes Tracy's bottom. 'The head's crowned,' she says.

   'Come on, Tracy, you have to roll over,' they beg.

   'I can't,' she says.

'You must,' they order. They're trying to help her turn over. Suddenly a head pops out, suspended between her legs. The midwife called Kathy is removing the slimy casing from its face and sucking out its mouth then the body is expelled in a slither of bloody mucous together with Tracy's delighted deep-throated groan.

I've heard that groan before. I remember wondering if it was me making that weird sound thirty or more years ago but no one I cared about was there.

A clamp is placed on the cord and the baby, still linked to her inside, is handed to Tracy. She clucks and croons over her son. 'Look at his doodle,' she says proudly to Tony. The blue-backed pads have been replaced by a green drop sheet. It's covered with bright iridescent orange blood surrounding the stainless steel bowl containing the dark rich purplish red sausage-like placenta criss-crossed with greenish rope-like strands.

Tracy torn and gaping open. 'The doctor will stitch it up later,' they say. While Tony inspects, prods and pokes the placenta, I have a brief nurse of my fifteen-minute-old grandson.

The Things They Do to Dear (Part 2)

Urodynamics is the name — sticking catheters in your ureter vagina and anus is the game.

> *anile*: of or like a weak old woman (L. *anilis* from *anus* old woman)   *Macquarie Concise Dictionary*

The nurse does the preparation then the specialist takes over. First we're going to fill your bladder with a radioactive dye. He points to a plastic container which he links to one of Dear's catheters. He undoes the stopper and the plastic pack sways gently on its chromed metal stand. Is there a pump, or is it just gravity propelling the fluid?

'Tell me when it becomes uncomfortable.'

'Now.'

'Just a little more, Dear.'

As Dear's bladder is artificially inflated she can hear the nurse clicking through the program on the Apple Mac. Bed is raised higher. Bed is raised lower.

'Don't move, hold your breath, I'm taking some X-rays.' *Snap.* 'Now this way, now that.' Dear is lying naked from the waist down hooked up to a Macintosh. Suddenly she's one with the machine. Security shattered when Dear looks at his full frontal lead apron.

'Now just keep still...' and suddenly a motor whirrs. Bed and Dear, complete with intrusive catheters, majestically trundle to an upright position. Fritz Lang's *Metropolis.* Dear decides she's feeling pretty crook. She didn't have her feet flat on the end of her bed and almost tips over in the turn around. The specialist and nurse think she's going to faint and make a grab for her. She tells them she is okay but wants to go to the toilet right now, please. 'No, Dear, we have to take more X-rays.' *Snap click. Snap click.*

'Now Dear, put your legs apart, bend your knees slightly and urinate.'

Dear reacts in horror. 'I can't — not standing up like this.'

'You must.'

I can't you will she doesn't and so they turn on taps and talk about running water and waterfalls and put Dear's hands into cold water until she wets herself standing up and bursts into tears. 'Thanks, Dear.'

Then the specialist takes Dear into a small room the size of a toilet with a chair just like a small birthing bed. Knees up Mother Brown and he sits with his face level with Dear's fundamental orifice, as her mother used to say, and pokes and prods.

Dear tries to pretend she is somewhere else. 'Get dressed, Dear, and we'll see you same time next week.'

More tests. Dear signs the consent form and so to hospital in July.

7 July 1994

It was my fourth visit to Jamieson. I didn't complain when I didn't get the private room I'd requested a month before. I found out later it had gone to someone who had complained. By 5.30 pm I was tucked into the two-bed ward listening to the quiet moans and groans penetrating the grey curtain. Her operation had been that morning. I tried to block out the sounds and longed for the privacy I wanted. At 7 pm the anaesthetist arrived. We'd met once or twice before. Stethoscope. Breathe in and out. Health history. How much do you weigh how much alcohol do you drink how often how many analgesics do you take.

He explains the procedure, says he's going to use a PCA for pain management and that I will have control of the dosage of pethidine via an intravenous tube. He smiles and leaves. Then the surgeon arrives. 'We'll have to stop meeting like this,' I try to joke. He's wearing a navy Bermuda jacket. I ask if he enjoyed his week on the ski slopes. 'Great,' he said and I hope he is well rested and that his hands are steady, because I realise he's getting older too. He has a kind face and thick grey wavy hair. He explains the procedure again in detail, and reminds me I will be placed on a drip and have a catheter in for four days. I decide not to have the sleeping tablet he prescribes 'if necessary'.

'I'll see you tomorrow afternoon.'

I lie and listen to the shift changes, staff bustling, patients using the toilet opposite. Their bodily odours mingle with food aromas emanating from the kitchen. Corridor lights on all night. Night sister checks regularly shining her torch. 'Are you awake, dear — everything all right, dear?'

The woman in the next bed moans most of the night. My surgery is scheduled for 2 pm so just before 6 am I'm given a cup of tea and a biscuit then nil by mouth. At lunch time my room companion has her first cooked meal. Food glorious food.

The Things They Do to Dear (Part 3)

Sister arrives with a safety razor and removes the thinning pubic hair. 'Have you used your bowels today, Dear?'

Dear expects a pre-surgical enema but sister says they don't do that any more. Dear, remembering pre-childbirth enemas, breathes a sigh of relief. 'Have a shower, put on this gown and cap, leave your panties off, take off your rings and pop your dentures into this bowl and pop back into bed. Then we'll give you a pre-med injection after which you mustn't get out of bed.' Dear hasn't slept and is anxious. The bed is clammy with protective plastic. The operation is delayed until 3 pm. Dear lies quietly contemplating the ceiling.

A male ward attendant arrives and converts the bed into a trolley. The rattling trip to theatre begins. Dear's eye is a camera watching the ceiling roll past. Swinging doors clip side of bed. Arrival. Eyes and masks begin to introduce themselves. 'Hi, I'm Julie. I'm your theatre sister today. Could you tell me your name and why you are here?' Dear is reminded of Pizza Hut and apologises for her toothless speech. 'Just lift your bottom, dear, and hop across to the operating table.' Dear's eye camera stares up at the encompassing circle of metallic bright lightedness. Stainless steel instruments and bowls arrayed beside eyes and masks, 'This will just be a small prick in your left hand,' and the swirling slides into oblivion.

Take deep breaths. 'Come on, keep breathing, Dear, Dear, it's all over.' Somehow Dear feels something is wrong. She can hear them talking about her. They are saying that every time they take the oxygen off she stops breathing. Take deep breaths, Dear, come on now. Dear experiences a lot of little deaths but there isn't any long tunnel with someone greeting her at the end like her Aunt Anne in Parkes once said after her heart attack. But Dear thinks about her Uncle Bill, who died of bowel cancer, sharpening the carving knives on the foot pedalled grinding stone in the chook yard where the huge lucerne tree was and he'd spit on the stone and grind first one side then the other. She remembers her cousin Ted lopping off the head of a Rhode Island Red on the chopping block in the woodshed. The body ran around and around looking for its head and she was about eight and Ted put her head on the chopping block and said he was going to chop her head off but he didn't.

Where am I?

THE LIFE AND LOVES OF AN XY WOMAN

Katherine Cummings

Here's the life ...

I was born nine years ago at the age of fifty-two years. Not born again; not reborn, just born. I had a long gestation period and a difficult one, full of pain and joy, achievement and failure. I jumped because I was pushed, but if I hadn't been pushed I think I would have jumped anyway. So I adopted the butterfly as my symbol. I emerged from the confining chrysalis of masculinity to be the female person I had always known myself to be, despite years of avoidance, denial and sublimation.

Sometimes my friends tell me the butterfly is not the symbol for me. It is too fragile and delicate. I always reply that *my* butterfly has teeth and claws and the will to use them. I thought this was an original conceit until someone sent me a newspaper clipping about a carnivorous South American butterfly that preys on ants. Nature always has the last laugh.

But it isn't easy being a woman without having had a childhood or teenage years. There is always a sense of something missing, and the mind tries to compensate in strange ways.

Sometimes, with no intent to deceive, I hear myself saying, 'When *I* was a little girl, I ...' and I pull myself up and examine this false memory that has been created from my knowledge of other women's childhoods, or from childhoods absorbed from my sister's storybooks and from my earliest longing to be female. There is a deep underlying desire in me for a complete life but this is something I will never have.

In a way I am lucky that so much of my childhood was spent in other countries as the family followed my seafaring father around the world. Eventually the time came when I set out on my own explorations and divagations. Lacunae and dislocations are inevitable in any account of my life; discrete groups of friends around the world who will never know each other. To visit them now is to step through windows into chunks and slices of a lifetime that bear no relationship to the other chunks and slices. My school friends, my university chums, my naval comrades, my professional colleagues, my Internet contacts ... maybe I will string them all together one day, like a sequence of amber beads through which I can cloudily view the trapped insects, fern leaves and raindrops of my life.

Perhaps the teenage years are hardest to be without. These should have been my apprenticeship years, time to explore sexuality and hairstyle, fashion and feminism, music and mankind, a meld of yearning for the security of being younger, of impatience for the adventure of being older ... years for comparing notes with one's peers, experimenting with life, whispering in corners, conspiring behind books. Years for listening to the tribal elders and appearing to scoff and disregard but really storing up their wisdom for the future.

This lack of an adolescence may account for the fact that my first few months of life as a woman were overlaid with a desperate attempt to catch up on all the things I had never known and all the experiences I had missed. 'Teenager in fast-forward' is sometimes used to describe this phase in transgendered people, and it seems appropriate. Into a few months I crammed all the hair, make-up, fashion, sexual politics and social dynamics that other women absorb as teenagers without knowing they are doing it.

Of course I made mistakes. I was past fifty but I desperately wanted to savour the learning years I had never known. My fast-forward efforts resulted in clothing and make-up styles inappropriate to my age and position. My heels were too high, my skirts too narrow, my necklines too low. I should have known better. If I *could* blush I *would* blush.

Can't I blush? Well, I *don't* blush. It may be due to the years of self-control which trained me to live two lives intermittently yet not make inappropriate gestures or respond to the 'wrong' name if I heard it in public. Those years when I lived between genders, sublimating my need to be a woman by playing at it with accommodating friends from time to time.

But I can certainly *cry*.

For forty years I never cried, but now I break down and sob to racking, hiccuping excess over personal distress, a friend's unhappiness or a sentimental passage of music. It must be the hormones. Every transgendered person asked to account for a behavioural quirk says, 'It's the hormones.'

For two years I lived as a probationary woman, learning to walk, talk, move and gesture all over again, like the victim of a terrible accident who must learn again how to cope with life or an amnesia victim painstakingly relearning all the facts she once knew so well, working through the *Britannica* and able to answer any question starting with the letters A to D. Next week she will also know things starting with E to H.

Learning to live in a gender role is like learning a language. If you do it from infancy it is simple, if you start when you are an adult there is a great deal to unlearn as well as a thousand new things to absorb.

In a way I *was* the victim of a terrible accident. I was born with XY chromosomes but some unpredictable hormonal wash during pregnancy (the flavour-of-the-month theory to account for transgenderism) created a need to be female in the deepest recesses of my psyche.

During my transition time between starting my new life and submitting my body to the surgeon's knife I was treated with great compassion and understanding by my local community, by my profession and by society at large. Only my family failed me, and they were simply demonstrating that problems obey the laws of perspective — up close they look bigger. They had most to lose and probably felt most betrayed by this strange quirk which was in me from birth, but suppressed and sublimated for the sake of others for two-thirds of my predicted life span. The loss of my wife and two of my three daughters was a tragic experience, but the alternative was suicide and I could not see that as a desirable solution on any terms, mine or theirs. Mind you, I didn't take a vote ...

Gradually I became more practised at the skills of womanhood. I dressed more appropriately and stopped buying from charity shops, and I learned that a five-minute make-up job is often more suitable for everyday life than a two-hour make-over. Unless I had a reason to 'dress up' I wore jeans and shirts and flat-heeled shoes like other women I knew. I felt myself blending into society in a way which was not only more appropriate but also more comfortable — for me *and* for society.

And gradually, too, I became more womanly in a physical sense. My hormone replacement therapy changed me. My skin became softer and curves appeared where bones and angles had been before. Some transgendered people have problems with HRT, and complain of side effects like headaches, nausea, cramps. I never had any side effects. There were, however, noticeable front effects though.

After two years the day came when I entered St David's private hospital for what the authorities call, on the form which lets me have a passport with an 'F' in the gender box, 'irreversible gender reassignment surgery'.

Did the operation make me a woman?

No.

I have always been a woman. But we all live inside our own heads and I will never know if my XY chromosome self-perception of womanhood is the same as that of XX chromosome women, or for that matter XXY chromosome women (Klinefelter's syndrome) or XXXY chromosome women (Caroline Cossey). But at least the operation made me *look* more like a woman. I could go to the beach without making painful arrangements to conceal inappropriate bits of my anatomy, I could join other women in the change rooms of gymnasia and aerobics classes without unease on their part or mine.

What *is* a woman? That is much more difficult to answer, because there are social, legal, grammatical and personal definitions and they tend to change from day to day. Nobody owns a word and sometimes the same word can be used in twenty different ways by twenty different people.

Justice Lockhart of the Federal Court stated in a recent judgment that in his opinion, a person who has had gender reassignment surgery from male to female is female and a woman, and a person who has had gender reassignment surgery from female to male is male and a man.

Hooray for Justice Lockhart! His statement does not change the law but it is *obiter dicta* and could be referred to in any future case where the gender of a post-operative transsexual is to be determined. And it flies in the face of Ormrod J's *Corbett v. Corbett* ruling, of which more anon.

I was, as I say, well treated by my various communities, but were there any noticeable changes in the way I was seen by friends and colleagues? Did I find people treating me differently in my female persona? Were my opinions overridden by men in conversation? Was I patronised by strangers? Was it assumed I was weaker than I had been, that my reading tastes had changed, that my skill at driving a car was suddenly in question?

In some cases this is exactly what happened, although my butterfly would sometimes show its teeth and claws on these occasions. I was upset, however, by the realisation that I had not observed these social handicaps more clearly from the other side of the gender barrier. I had prided myself on treating men and women equally before my transition, yet I found that even my eyes had been clouded by testosterone, and some of my attitudes had bordered on the paternalistic. I try now to make amends by joining in the struggle for recognition of a woman's place as an equal; not a servant, nor an ornament nor a toy.

Oddly enough, some of those who might be assumed to have an interest in elevating women are those who seem to wish to preserve the status quo.

I went to a speech therapist because I was tired of being called 'Sir' on the telephone and she explained that it was not simply a matter of pitch and timbre and vocabulary but also of cadence. 'A woman,' she explained, 'finishes her sentences with a terminal rise.'

I could hardly believe my ears. Not only was the terminal rise of fairly recent origin (it did not generally exist when I went away to the United States in 1968 although it was firmly entrenched in the schools when I returned in 1973) but it was a speech characteristic I had fought to stamp out in my daughters. The terminal rise seemed to me to be a constant request for affirmation and approval, a tentative mode of address that virtually sought permission to express an opinion. 'Stop asking me questions,' I would say to my daughters when their voices rose at the end of each sentence, 'Make statements!'

I found my memories and attitudes of masculinity gradually being submerged by new perceptions, feelings and attitudes so that second nature became first nature and my former existence became a vagueness that had to be focused on with considerable effort before it became a reality, rather like the formless dreams we try so hard to see clearly before we wake, and that always move beyond the periphery of vision. I knew there had been a person in my former existence who still loved and wanted his ex-wife and who missed his children desperately, yet the perceptions, emotions and experiences of my female persona were starting to overlay the blurring memories of my male self and to achieve the colours and sharp edges of immediacy.

My female self was becoming real life, my male self was becoming a memory.

Now for the loves ...

A quick and stupid assumption holds that a man who becomes a woman does so in order to make love to men. There are all kinds of foolish theories that label transgendered people as homosexuals unable to admit the fact and evading what they see as a stigma by the simple (!) solution of gender reassignment. Since many, even most, transgenders are aware of their gender dysphoria in infancy, this seems like a farfetched notion. That a four-year-old can be aware enough of sexuality and the differences between genders to settle monomaniacally on a course which will allow him or her to grow up and make love to her/his own gender by way of surgical intervention is rather too foolish to countenance.

Unfortunately one of the foolish people who held this view of transgenderism was Justice Ormrod, who presided over *Corbett v. Corbett* (1969) in which April Ashley's husband Arthur Corbett sought an annulment of their marriage on the grounds that April Ashley had been born male. This was the first test in a British court of the right of a transsexual to marry. Ormrod ruled that April Ashley was male despite her reassignment, and *Corbett v. Corbett* has laid its dead hand on British and Australian law affecting transsexuals ever since.

Recent correspondence from Ormrod to an Australian jurist currently carrying out a study on the place of transsexuals in society has demonstrated Ormrod's total lack of understanding of gender dysphoria as he maunders on about how satisfactory anal sex is and wonders that anyone would want a vagina in order to have sex.

I became quite choleric when I read this correspondence and wrote a series of sharp comments to my jurist friend. Very few male-to-female transsexuals seek gender reassignment in order to go to bed with men. We seek reassignment for our own peace of mind and the thought of anal sex would be repugnant to most. The thought of going through life with male genitals would be totally insupportable to virtually all. How could we bear to look at ourselves every day, half-and-half parodies of humanity, female above, male below?

So then, what of my own sexuality? I am what I call a 'second-wave' transsexual, one who fought to suppress my gender dysphoria and tried to live as others wanted me to be. For one-third of my life I lived to please my parents. Then I married (thinking this might redeem me from my mad desire to be female), raised three lovely daughters and finally gave way (after some conflict with my family who wanted me to abjure my insane daydreams) to my need to be a woman, finally and forever. 'First wave' transsexuals, like April Ashley and Caroline Cossey, move across the gender border much earlier in their lives and live virtually their whole adult lives in the female role (I hope female-to-male transsexuals who read this account will forgive my concentration on my own situation and not theirs. It becomes insupportably complex to frame every sentence to cover both sides of the mirror image). It is 'first-wave' transsexuals who are most likely to want sex with men. Those of us who follow later in life more often than not retain our original sexual orientation. I sometimes say that my surgeon made me a lesbian.

My surgical reassignment did not affect my love for my family. I would have returned to my wife on almost any terms, as lover; as best friend; as roommate. But her repugnance for my condition was such that she first divorced me, then sought annulment of our marriage.

The annulment is a story in itself. I had assumed the Catholic Church might have moved into the twentieth century in terms of understanding the human psyche, but in fact the Catholic tribunal that controlled our annulment was as cruel, dishonest and secretive as the Spanish Inquisition. Evidence was called but never shown to the parties to the annulment, so that nothing could be challenged, and I was never allowed to hear any of the deliberations, although I requested this right. All evidence was written up in the judgment without attribution so that it was effectively anonymous. I was allowed to see the judgment only after the tribunal had ruled in favour of annulment and my appeal against that ruling had been dismissed.

The judgment was full of lies and irrelevancies, including the evidence from some unidentified person that when I cross-dressed it was in order to be attractive to men. A blatant lie. It was suggested that I owned 135 pairs of shoes, making me the Imelda Marcos of Balmain. Another lie, but even if true, what possible relevance could that have to the moment of marriage, the only moment which is relevant in an annulment proceeding? The grounds given for the annulment were that I had shown gross lack of discretion in marrying. If this means anything in the English language it means that I should have realised when I took my marriage vows that twenty-three years later I would be forced by circumstance into leaving the marriage and seeking gender reassignment.

How foolish of me not to have known that!

Incidentally my attempts to have civil liberties lawyers take on the Catholic Church in defence of my rights have failed miserably. Letters have not been answered, telephone calls not returned. They couldn't be running scared just because I want them to sue the Pope, surely? Even my butterfly has sharper teeth than they.

I have said in another place that gender dysphoria is a medical condition. (If it is not, why is it treated by the medical profession, i.e. psychiatrists, endocrinologists, surgeons?) Yet we are treated as if we make a wilful choice to endure all the pain and expense; as if transsexualism were a whim, or a hobby, or a sexual perversion.

I was left in a limbo of loving, still wanting my wife, still missing my children. One of my daughters stood by me. The other two didn't want to know me. For five years I stood aloof from the world of sex, hoping against hope that my wife would wake up one morning to a new realisation of my worth and return to me. I admit my hopes were eroded by her marriage to the Catholic who had been the instigator of the annulment.

Incidentally, although I had certainly not sought gender reassignment in the hope of having sex with a man, or men, I have never denied that this is a possibility. I did not know how much difference might be wrought on my libido by my regimen of hormones, nor did I know what social and psychological changes might occur in my life. So I did not rule out the possibility that Mr Right would come along and sweep me off my feet like the recycled virgin I was. The closest I ever came to this was when a Telecom technician young enough to be my son accosted me in a bookshop and asked me where I was going next. I *was* rather fetchingly dressed in a peasant blouse, straight skirt and high heels (during my fast forward period) but I stammered something about going back to work and scuttled away from the pickup scene as fast as I could, skirt and heels notwithstanding.

Then one day I took a closer look at my empty emotional life and admitted that my wife would never come back to me, even if her egregious husband were somehow removed from the scene, and I should stop moping and think about the rest of my life. I should no longer reject the idea of finding a new partner.

No sooner had I made this decision than someone came into my life, almost miraculously, following a series of coincidences which would be laughed off the stage as the most blatant use of *deus ex machina*. I found myself in the company of an intelligent, witty, warm and wonderful woman who shared many of my literary enthusiasms and enjoyed my company. Within a few weeks I had declared my love for her, and, although she was startled at my boldness, she had the grace to take me seriously and we commenced a close and loving relationship which endured for a year. It might well have endured longer had she not remembered one day that she is heterosexual and we parted tearfully, but lovingly, and are still close friends.

I was still not convinced I was attracted only to women, and was prepared to seek out a partner first and find out his or her sex later. I have never been sex-mad. I would rather have fine food than sex and good conversation than either.

I had a brief fling with a pre-operative transsexual during a trip I took through the United States. What I had thought to be a two-way attraction turned out to be almost exclusively in my head and the relationship foundered when we parted. 'Aha!' I hear the Religious Right crying triumphantly, 'So she *is* a homosexual by her own admission! Oops! I mean *his* own admission!' Sorry, folks. As far as I am concerned, my partner in the States is a woman, just as I was a woman long, long before surgery, so the most I will confess to is that we were lesbians. But I'm sure that will do. Damnation is damnation, after all. If you believe in that sort of nonsense.

When I came back to Australia, having been rejected by

my American playmate, I found myself drifting into a closer and closer relationship with one who shares many of my interests, including writing. She is the published author of many books and an independent spirit of great courage, brilliance and physical beauty. There is an age discrepancy between us but there has been a similar discrepancy in all my post-marital relationships, and as I intend to live forever, this hardly matters.

She is currently undergoing a lot of ignorant criticism from her family who see me as a kind of psycho-sexual Svengali, luring her to the surgical table. They blandly overlook the fact that I would never have met her if she had not been already well down the track to St David's.

And so my life proceeds. I have written one full-length autobiography (which I am proud to say won the Human Rights Award for non-fiction in 1992) and yet so much has happened since then that I feel I should add a lengthy epilogue before it appears again. I closed off my book in the belief that I could never love again. How wrong I was! I have also discovered the Internet and am in contact with some hundreds of intelligent, articulate transsexuals and transgendered people in several different countries. From them I have learned a great deal I never knew, for I found my way down the difficult path of transsexualism virtually alone, forming my own opinions and accepting the strictures of the medical profession as if they really knew something. I have modified many of my opinions since I wrote my autobiography and will probably continue to do so.

What has emerged most clearly is the primitive stage Australia occupies in recognising the legal and human rights of transsexuals. We cringingly follow *Corbett v. Corbett*, ignoring the many attacks made by sensible members of the legal profession on the narrow-minded bigotry of Ormrod J., and we fail to understand that the major question is not 'Why should transsexuals be accorded the same rights as anyone else?' but rather 'Why should transsexuals not be accorded the same rights as everyone else?' Who would be harmed if we were permitted to marry in our gender of choice? Who would suffer if we could have our documentation altered to conform to our new personae? The dead hand of religion imposes laws dreamed up by timorous Middle Eastern nomads afraid of thunderstorms and earthquakes three thousand years ago and we do not have the moral courage to discard superstitions that should no longer have anything to do with modern societal rules. New Zealand has made much greater progress than we in the liberalisation of laws concerning transsexuals.

I do what I can, as an XY woman. I write to politicians. I speak at gender conferences. I write for publication. I stand up to be counted. I do not expect to make much difference in my lifetime, but we have to start somewhere. Gender reassignment surgery is just over forty years old (Christine Jorgensen's operation in 1952 was the first successful one to be publicised). In that time remarkable progress has been made in recognising legal and human rights of transsexuals in Holland, some of the Scandinavian countries, New Zealand and parts of the United States and Canada. Why is Australia so backward? I realise the Liberals blame the National Party, but surely that can't be the whole story. Why should wide hats and narrow minds disadvantage a whole innocent sub-group of society who want nothing more than to get on with their reordered lives?

Of course there are good people (like my jurist friend) working for more humane treatment of transsexuals in Australia. With luck this account of the brief life and unexpected loves of an XY woman may inform a few more lay people, as my earlier book did.

It has been a remarkable nine years for me, since first I wrote to my colleagues at the college where I worked, telling them what I intended to do with what was left of my life.

It has been such an adventure that I sometimes tell my friends I have a mind to go back the other way, just for the interest and the challenge.

Ah, well. Maybe not. Once may be enough.

ABOUT TIME

by Jane Seifert

Sixteen from sixty — that's forty-four. Then there were
eight years back in New Zealand after I was married —
that's thirty-six. Then two years in the 1970s and two more
years just recently, living in London, and another year
back in Wellington nursing my sister. So now we're down
to thirty-one — still more than half my life. Can I really
still call New Zealand home? Am I really a New Zealander
or that peculiar hybrid, a 'Kiwaussie', which is what Brian
sometimes calls himself? I return to visit family and
friends every year or so and feel comfortable there but
know in my heart that I will not, could not, return to live.
My children all live here; my grandchildren too. I have a
context here within which my life revolves and it is of the
here and now, not past history. The past enriches the present but is not enough to live on, to provide my daily diet.
So what am I? Who am I? Should I be an Australian?

Music filtered from the trees in the corner and I looked at
the three musicians. All in jeans, T-shirts, boots, Akubras
stuck well back on their heads, their fingers flying over
guitar strings or lips pursed behind mouth organs as they
tried to respond to my request to play 1930s music. It was
not quite as I had planned it, but it was very Australian. I
leaned in the doorway with my glass of champagne and
quietly surveyed the guests. They were mainly Australian

but some had come originally from India, Canada, New Zealand and England and, as far as I knew, those immigrants were all now Australian citizens. How did they feel? Were their hearts still back 'home'? How had they come to this country and why? When did they decide to become citizens — after five years? ten years? twenty?

I remember how I came that first time, and why. It was January 1951. My mother and stepfather and their one-year-old son had come here the year before and were living in Cooma where my stepfather was a surveyor on the Snowy Mountains Hydro-Electric Scheme, one of a team of experienced engineers, surveyors, drillers, tunnellers who came from New Zealand with Bill Hudson, later Sir William, the Snowy Mountains Authority Commissioner. I had to finish school in New Zealand but then I told my father I was off. No thanks or regrets, this was my chance for adventure. I had no thought for the future; I had no plans at all.

I was just sixteen. After an eight-hour flight from Evans Bay, Wellington, I was almost unable to breathe for nervous excitement as the flying-boat came in over Sydney Harbour and breasted gently to a stop in Rose Bay. I struggled to assume a sophisticated air as if I was quite used to international air travel and not overly impressed with the blue sky, sparkling harbour, the city I had seen glittering round its shores and over the hills and far away. But all pretence was thrown aside when I saw my mother and rushed into her arms with tears of relief and joy.

We stayed for a week at the Bondi Pacific Hotel where the trams rattled past to the terminus and the fire escapes at the back led directly onto the beach. One night there was a power failure and the manager brought candles round. Before bed I approached the hand basin in our room, candlestick held aloft to put on the shelf but instead, with a loud scream, I dropped it in the basin, right on top of the biggest and surely the most ferocious centipede in the world. At this stage my mother had not thought to tell me about snakes, spiders and other interesting creatures abounding in the Australian bush. Which is probably just as well.

It being January and Sydney, it rained. An aunt I had never met — wife to my mother's much older brother — arranged to take me to lunch in the city. I had spent the past eight years at boarding school and had few clothes apart from my uniform, which I had vowed (uselessly) never to wear again. My Aunt Rose volunteered to buy me a summer frock and a raincoat. I accepted her generous offer because I really needed and wanted those clothes, but my feelings were very confused. I was embarrassed by her, and felt guilty because I was embarrassed. At both the primary and secondary boarding schools I had attended, the teachers were English and had a strong influence on my speech and attitudes. My natural colonial vowels had been modified to a more English sound. I had been madly in love with my history teacher, Norah Pennington, who had pale skin, dark hair and eyes, and dressed superbly in well-cut suits of finest English tweed with toning Pringle twinsets. Aunt Rose, this day, was wearing a brightly coloured, floral patterned, *nylon* dress with *white* shoes. What was even worse, she possessed what I thought of as a Sydney accent: nasal and twanging and rather loud. My sensibilities suffered — from her appearance, her voice, her generosity.

I was relieved to get on the train to Cooma. The countryside seemed very dry and dusty, the sheep dirty, the sun merciless in the cloudless sky. It was very different from the lush green dairy farming country of the Manawatu, where even on the finest summer day clouds drifted over the Ruahine ranges. There were more surprises when we reached Cooma, which was quite unlike the small country towns I knew back home. By 1951, Cooma was a roaring frontier town, divided into the old and the new. The old, the members of the Monaro farming community and the townspeople, struggled to adjust to the sudden influx of Snowy workers, who were mainly young single men, refugees from a battered Europe. Through the week the Snowy workers lived in camps in places with odd names like Smiggins Hole and Island Bend, but at the weekend they came to town, their pay in hand and often with the other hand clenched in a fist or holding a knife. There were historical scores to settle, new slights to avenge and nothing much else to do in this dry hole at the bottom of the world. Between the two groups were those wanting to retain their old clients while seeing opportunities by serving the well-paid New Australians. The bush telegraph went into overdrive the day the newsagent put a sign in his window saying 'German spoken here'.

I needed a job. I needed money for clothes and to pay some rent to my mother, but I had just left school and had no skills or training. Shorthand and typing was the answer, of course, so off I went to the Brigidine convent where the nuns obliged with the only commercial courses available. Businesses were accustomed to phoning the convent when they wanted junior staff, and that is how I came to be the invoice typist at Hibberd's garage, the largest dealer of new and used cars in town. There were four women in that office upstairs above the car yards, and we used to have competitions looking down on the ranks of cars and guessing the make and model of each one. With games like that and making tea, I got a little bored. I also wanted to earn more than three pounds a week; after paying rent I had thirty shillings to spend.

The Snowy Mountains Authority (SMA) needed teachers of English. With such a polyglot workforce there had to be a common language of communication, especially for safety purposes. They advertised and I, blithely confident in my ignorance, went along to an interview. Yes, they could hear I spoke English and had a reasonable vocabulary. Would I please just do a written test? That was it. Looking back I am not sure who to feel sorry for — myself or the men I was supposed to teach.

There were generally fifteen to twenty in my two evening classes each week. Ages ranged from about twenty to nearly sixty; at least the Russian with the lovely smile, brilliant blue eyes and snow-white hair looked old to me but he was probably in his early fifties, as the Snowy was no place for old men. This man (I can hardly call any of them students nor myself a teacher) smiled and nodded at me most graciously but apart from learning my name and saying 'hello' and 'goodbye' each evening I cannot believe that I taught him any English. There were no resources. I used newspapers, magazines, anything I could find, gave them vocabulary lists to learn, tried to explain the confusing and contradictory rules of spelling and pronunciation and tried not to interrupt too often when they read aloud in halting, stumbling accents.

They were all older than me, yet I felt in some way responsible for them. The younger men treated me with friendly diffidence or gentle courtesy so I never felt threatened by the situation. I walked into the last class that year to find the room decorated with balloons and streamers and a big 'thank you and goodbye' message on the blackboard. There was no class that evening but there were songs accompanied by accordion or mouth organ, a few attempts to teach me some folk dances which ended with all concerned collapsing with giggles and laughter, some dreadful *vino* (sic) and some very interesting food, got I don't know where. More than forty years later, my memory of that night is still vivid. I think about it with wonder, awe and delight. Perhaps because I too was a newcomer to Australia, I identified with those men coming to start a new life in this strange and often forbidding land. Perhaps they excused my youth and lack of expertise because they understood I had done my best and, for that night at least, we were all sharing in positively Panglossian hopes for the future.

My immediate future, as it turned out, was not to be so bright. I became pregnant: not a good thing to be in the 1950s. For a seventeen-year-old there were only three options: marriage, abortion or hiding away, then having the baby adopted out. I would not have married the father under any circumstances as I understood much later that I was raped. At the time I did not even know what rape meant, so that I felt the whole sordid incident was my fault and I hated myself and hated the man. He was a young German from one of the camps whom I met through the social club organised by the Young Anglicans. He was always pestering me, asking me to go out. I had a boyfriend — a true-blue Aussie named George. Tall, dark and handsome, he affected an Errol Flynn moustache and I thought he was wonderful. He was an apprentice carpenter, browned by working outdoors, lean and fit from sport, laconic and kind and gentle. When I had my appendix out he scandalised the matron by getting me to make dry flies so that my pristine white bedcover was scattered with multicoloured feathers and tiny silver hooks glittered on the floor. He taught me to cast a line and I caught my first trout in the Murrumbidgee, which he then cooked over our campfire under the gum trees. Most unusually for a young Australian male of the time, he knitted. He was completely unselfconscious about it, making up elaborate patterns for his ski jumpers: deer and fir trees, kangaroos on skis, complicated abstracts.

George was never my lover although I think he might have been eventually. If the child had been his, I would have wanted to marry him. As it was I could not even face telling him. I just wanted to slink away and curl up and die in a hole like a wounded animal. I had no money for an abortion and nobody to turn to for help. The thought of telling my mother was even worse than the thought of telling George. Finally, when I was more than three months 'gone', I went to our doctor. He surprised me by being kind, thoughtful and helpful. He uttered no words of condemnation, gave no sermons, did not patronise. He was practical. He was the same doctor who had taken my appendix out some time before, leaving me with the smallest, neatest appendix scar from only three stitches. I praise him now; I couldn't then. He took me home and helped me find the strength to tell my mother and stepfather; he made arrangements for me to go to Hopewood House at Bowral.

After giving out information that I was going home to nurse my sister and suffering a round of farewells that I found so painful as to be almost unbearable, I finally arrived in Bowral in August — late winter. Even after Cooma it was cold and at Hopewood House it was colder than elsewhere. Not because the people there were unkind, but we 'fallen' girls were already chilled by the circumstances of our being there, and besides the supervisor was a fresh-air fiend, so we had to sleep with all the windows open even on the frostiest nights. I would get up at six in the morning, dress and go to the kitchens for breakfast duty — we all worked for our keep, helping with orphaned and abandoned children. Some days I think my fingers and toes never thawed out. I suffered terrible chilblains. The gardens there were lovely and as summer came the roses bloomed and I spent as much time as could be found, reading in the rose garden. Apart from my mother I wrote to hardly anyone as it meant a tissue of lies that I could not cope with, but my mother had written to my father in New Zealand and he asked me to go home when I could. I cried with utter relief when I read his letter. I knew I was a grave disappointment to him.

In January 1953 I gave birth to a daughter and thereby contributed to Australia's postwar population growth. I gave her up for adoption. I do not know what became of my daughter; there has never been any contact. But this did not bind me to Australia; on the contrary. I rushed back to New Zealand as soon as possible and my tall tale turned true when my sister asked me to live with her and her husband and nine-year old son. While I had conceived too easily and given birth so naturally after an easy pregnancy, my sister had suffered miscarriages. The answer was complete bed rest and I was the godsent one to make this possible.

That was a difficult year. I juggled shopping, cooking, cleaning, the care of my nephew and a full-time job as invoice typist at SKF Ballbearing Co., Wellington. My sister's pregnancy kept my own experience too freshly in my mind; her fear of yet another miscarriage and her envy of my ease in creating a child caused tension between us which added to my misery. She gave birth to a son before Christmas and my duty was done. I decided to return to Australia.

This second time I came by boat on the *Monowai*. This time I brought some clothes and money, not having had much opportunity to shop or indulge in a social life for the past year and therefore having saved most of my wages. By this time my mother and stepfather had moved to Tasmania where my stepfather was working for the State Hydro-Electric Commission, based at the village of Tarraleah.

The administration manager and his wife, who lived next door, were good friends of my mother and stepfather. Through this connection I was able to get a job in the administration office which was extremely fortunate as there was really nowhere else to work and the alternative was to move down to Hobart to get a job. I worked for the paymaster, a Polish man who had flown with the RAF during the war. He was the first man I knew who used perfume and he always had a flower in his buttonhole, even if it sometimes had to be a native wildflower. I would bring him pinks from my mother's garden. He drank his tea from a glass set in an ornate silver holder.

On paydays I had to call out the men's names from the time charts and get them to sign for their pay envelope. Many Greeks worked there and they derived a great deal of amusement from my attempts to pronounce their multi-syllabic names with all those 'opoulopoulis' endings.

During the summer we played tennis and picnicked and swam at Lake St Clair. In winter it snowed. On one occasion I could not get to the office to work until the snowplough had been through. My mother's birthday was in August and she always wanted a picnic so off we would go into the snow-covered bush and my stepfather would light a fire with dry wood from the Land Rover and we would join hands round the fire and sing and shout 'Happy Birthday' until we shook snow from the gum trees. Once it even snowed on Christmas Eve. I came out of a party at a neighbour's up the street just before mid-night, going home to check on my young brother who had fallen asleep and been taken home to bed a couple of hours earlier. There was no wind and snowflakes were falling very softly and slowly, coming to rest so gently on the ground and sparkling in the street lights. There was nobody about — no footprints or tracks of any kind to spoil the illusion that I had stepped into a brand new world; a secret, magic world created just for me. I stood still in a kind of trance until somebody somewhere slammed a car door and I realised I was freezing.

One month later, I was comatose from the heat. We all lay on the floor of the Ozone Hotel in Perth, draped in wet towels while ceiling fans creaked above us. It was heatwave weather and the change was too much, too sud-den for all of us; that included my mother and stepfather, their young son, then almost six, my divorced older sister and her son aged about eleven who had joined us from New Zealand just before Christmas, and me. Plus our bitser dog. We had crossed from Melbourne to Perth by train over the previous three days and on arrival at Perth railway station at eight in the morning it was already over forty degrees Celsius. But worse was to come.

After my stepfather had signed his contract with the WA Lands and Survey Department, bought a utility truck and hired a couple of chainmen, he drove us to Yarloop, which made Cooma look like a sophisticated city and Tarraleah like the Garden of Eden. Yarloop is south and inland from Perth, a timber mill in the bush with a few houses standing forlornly either side of the access road. The afternoon we arrived it was over forty degrees; there was nobody there to greet us because everyone was out fighting a bushfire. We found the house that Lands and Survey had allocated to the family, climbed the ash-covered steps, crossed the verandah and opened the front door. Sand and grit swirled up through the gaps in the floorboards, geckos ran up the walls and flattened themselves against the ceilings, and the wood-fired stove leered at us as we walked through to open the back door. Then, and only then, my mother sat down on the back porch steps, laid her head on her folded arms and wept.

At the end of the long backyard with its token gum tree and bare earth like an old man's pate showing through the shrivelled grass, the bushfire roared like a wild beast. A row of men flailed sacks with an energy born of desperation and my stepfather ran to help. It was not a good beginning to life in the west. My sister got a bookkeeping job in the mill office and the children were bussed to a school somewhere, but there was nothing for me.

After a week I returned to Perth and found a room in a boarding house where I existed on Arnott's milk arrowroot biscuits and oranges and went every few days to a city hotel where I would brazenly walk upstairs as if I were a guest, find an empty bathroom and luxuriate in a bath for half an hour. I was terrified of the gas heater in the bathroom at the boarding house, with its spitting, huffing and knocking noises. The gas cooker was just as bad. It was in the hallway and its use was shared with other residents. It was always filthy and I preferred the biscuits and oranges. I got an office job and met Alan Bond. He had the sign-writing contract and came weekly to do the windows. He was like a bouncing ball, giving cheek to everyone. We all agreed he would never amount to anything because he was too cocky. I found a house in South Perth along the river near the golf course, and my relieved mother moved back to civilisation.

In the summer of 1954–55 I caught the last bus back from the city one night. The bus driver, a tall, blond Dutchman about ten years older than me, offered to drive the bus past the terminus to where I lived in Labouchere Road; he was concerned about my walking alone past the golf course so late at night. I was flattered by his concern and each time I got on his bus in the following weeks I gave him a 'thank you' smile. We did not speak again until one evening as I was getting off at the terminus, he asked whether I would like to go to a movie with him. And so began my relationship with the father of my second child.

There is still so much trauma attached to the next year — indeed the next three years of my life — that even now, nearly forty years on, it is hard for me to look objectively at that time or even think about it. It is hard to explain to myself, let alone anyone else, how ignorant I still was about sex, particularly about contraception. I became sexually neutral after the birth of my first child; did not want to be touched; generally disliked men; swore I would never marry. My parents had divorced when I was nine; my two older sisters were both divorced and both had unsuccessful second marriages. To me all this was bound together with men and their sexual appetites. Not that I did not have a sexual appetite of my own but, after my first pregnancy, fear had kept me safe.

The Dutchman and I became lovers that summer. I remember the first time, a weekend when the rest of the family were away, and him asking me, 'Is it safe?' I said yes, thinking he was worried that someone would walk in on us. Too late I understood he was asking me about contraception. The next two months were like the lull before the storm. I was happy, in love, life was wonderful.

Then the worry began and the tension grew and grew until the time for doubt and hope was past. I gave my lover the bad news, thinking that now was the time to cast aside my aversion to marriage and that perhaps all could still be well. His anger frightened me. I thought he would hit me. He accused me of trapping him; hadn't I told him it was safe? We fought every time we met. I could not understand his anger. Wasn't I the one in trouble, carrying the baby? I had loaned him money to get his car fixed; now I asked for it back as I was planning an abortion. He did not have enough to give me and did not see why he should repay it after I had trapped him so miserably.

Time was running out. Worry had caused me to lose weight but soon my mother would look at me and she would know. I could not put her through this again. I asked him for some money, any money, whatever he could spare, to help me go away — somewhere, anywhere. Then it came out. He had no spare money because he was already supporting a wife and child. I wanted to die. The love I had felt for him had long since melted away, my disillusionment was complete.

I told my mother some story or other and went to Adelaide. I applied for a clerical job in an insurance office but they required a medical and when I returned to the personnel manager I could see he had read the doctor's report. His response was typical of the way men so often see women, either as whores or saints. First he condemned me, berated me, called me a slut; then he propositioned me, wanting to have sex right there on his office floor. I do not know how I got myself out of that office, my legs were shaking so. I found a toilet down the corridor and vomited until there was nothing left to heave. I did not apply for jobs like that again. I took a job as a live-in housekeeper. My employees were a sixtyish businessman and his wife who was partially bedridden. They had a beautiful home at Beaumont in the Adelaide Hills with views down over the city lights. I cleaned and cooked and sometimes read to the wife. Her doctor visited her every other day and one day as he was leaving he asked whether I would come and see him at his surgery. The wife had seen I was pregnant and wanted me to leave.

That doctor, like the one in Cooma, was kind, considerate and practical. He found me another live-in position caring for a toddler whose single mum worked full-time. All went well until in early spring I caught the flu from the child's mother and could not shake it off. I was useless, unable to get out of bed long enough to mind the child properly. I was also nearly eight months pregnant and had no strength of mind to cope with what was ahead. I believe I took refuge in being in bed. The doctor phoned my mother, bought me a train ticket, drove me to the station and saw me into the carriage. He assured me my mother wanted to look after me. I did not believe him but was powerless to alter the course he had set me on. And he was right. Again.

A few weeks later my mother phoned for a taxi about midnight after I told her my waters had broken. She told the driver to take us quickly to the King Edward Hospital. We dissolved in hysterics when the taxi driver rushed along St George's Terrace and with squealing brakes pulled up outside the King Edward Hotel. My son was born at 7:30 the next morning — in King Edward Hospital. From the start everyone seemed to expect I would put him up for adoption. The social worker brought me the forms to sign before he was twenty-four hours old. My mother came and painted a gloomy scenario of our survival if I had to look after the two of us. I gave my son a name. That was not a good sign as far as the social worker was concerned; I was getting too attached. I told my mother I could not go around Australia having babies and giving them away; couldn't she understand? She immediately became supportive. She had merely been playing devil's advocate; we would manage somehow. She spoke to the social worker. She too then accepted my decision and suggested I try to get maintenance from the father.

It was a long, hot summer but I hardly noticed, so engrossed was I with my beautiful boy. Each day was a new adventure, a surprise, a delight. I even thought his crying was wonderful. I forgot myself; my son was everything and he needed me. When he was four months old I got a court hearing for the maintenance application. I went that morning with my mother beside me and the baby in my arms; I was breastfeeding so had to have him with me. I was shocked to find the Dutchman there, with his wife holding his hand. I cannot recall much of the hours spent at the courthouse but when I went to feed my son next morning my milk had dried up so there was nothing there for him. I cried. I never did get much maintenance; the payments would get behind until after about three months the father would get a summons and then serve a sentence of a week or so in lieu. That cleared his debt but did nothing for me, and off we went again.

When my son was six months old I decided I must go back to work. My mother was happy to care for him during the day. My brother was now eight years old and at school; my stepfather was working out in the wheat-belt somewhere and came home only once a month for a few days. I wanted a better paid, more interesting job than invoice typing so enrolled in a comptometry course with Burroughs. I topped the class for accuracy and speed and Burroughs gave me a glowing reference, which got me a job in the accounts department of H.M. Customs in Fremantle. I bought myself a Lambretta motor scooter to get quickly and easily from South Perth to work. My son walked at ten months and was running at twelve. He would hear the scooter coming down the hill behind our house and run to the side gate to greet me. I don't know who then got most excited as we hugged and kissed and danced around the lawn.

I loved my job, although I was the only female and had to put up with a lot of sexist jokes. The youngest male in the office was my age and forever patting me on the bottom as he passed. I asked him again and again not to do it as I found it offensive. He would just laugh. One day he patted me and I turned and flew at him, scratching his face with my nails. He never touched me again. I computed all the pays for H.M. Customs' employees; I worked on the excise figures for Kwinana, going there each month to read the gauges on the tanks, then working out the complicated formulas on the comptometer. When the bottom-patter wasn't around, I answered customs agents' requests for forms at the office counter. Two years later, when I married one of the young customs agents, the rumour was that his firm had about ten years' supply of our forms. They had been his excuse for visiting the office to see me. But this was eighteen months before I was aware of his interest in me; he was three years younger and I hardly recognised his existence.

Around Christmas 1958, the departmental head asked me if I was going to the New Year's Eve Customs ball but I said no; I did not have a partner. A little later he asked whether he could introduce me to someone who was interested in me; his wife was teaching this young man at night classes. It did not sound too promising but everyone else was going to the ball and I felt I would like to go too. Brian was a gangly young man with an inhibiting stammer, which is why he had been unable to approach me himself. I realised I had seen him many, many times in our office, getting those forms. We went to the beach on my motor scooter; we went to the movies and I took him home. We lived on opposite sides of Perth and had long phone conversations which my stepfather could not understand, but Brian took so long to get out a sentence. He took me out to dinner, to the King's Park restaurant where we sat on the terrace and I ordered a seafood cocktail which proved to be awful, but I didn't mind.

We went to the New Year's Eve ball. I found he could jive and I couldn't; I could waltz and foxtrot and tango and he couldn't. I was impressed, though, when he tucked into his carpet-bag steak, ignoring the floor show which had just started — a 'mermaid' undressing in a huge fish tank (it was still the fifties). We drove back to my place in the car he had borrowed, parked and talked until the sun came up over the Swan River. For the first time I told him about my son, but not quite everything, for I said I was divorced from his father. Brian asked to go inside to see him and stood for some time gazing at the sleeping boy. Not long after that he started asking me to marry him. All through that summer while we went to movies, swimming, and took my son with us on picnics, he talked of marriage. He was only twenty years old, with no prospects that I could see; he was an innocent, inexperienced with women, and yet with a faith in himself that I would have found touching if I hadn't found it so foolish.

To shut him up I played my trump card. I told him I had never been married; that I was a fallen woman. He laughed with relief. I had forgotten he was a Roman Catholic so divorce was a greater sin than a child born out of wedlock. I still said no but he had weakened my defences and he did have one great advantage: he loved and cared about my child. I knew he would be a good father and my mother was finding the two-year-old a handful now that she was fifty-seven.

We married on 6 June 1959, just six months after we first met. A week later we sailed to New Zealand on the

Oronsay to begin our married life. I, of course, had to leave work when I married; that is how it was then and for several years after. Brian had been told by his employer that if he was foolish enough to marry he could not expect an increase in wages to help him along. Apart from those financial considerations, his mother disliked me because I was older than her son, because I had a child, because she was losing control over Brian. For the next eight years we lived in New Zealand while Brian established his career in the computer industry, we had two more children, accumulated some assets, consolidated our marriage. It was a good move.

The third time I 'emigrated' to Australia I flew into Melbourne, all expenses paid, accompanied by my husband and three children. From that time on, although we were to have two stints living in London during the following twenty-five years, we always had a home in Australia to come back to and there was never any question of returning to live in New Zealand. We built a house in Melbourne but after only three years were moved to Sydney.

I took up copper enamelling, joined the committee of the local community centre, I drove my three children to soccer games, hockey games, to school friends' parties. I drove myself to drink. I came to see that I was not wholehearted about being a suburban mum. I did not play bridge or golf, I did not enjoy Melbourne Cup luncheon parties, I could not and would not participate in the key-swapping parties that were then popular. My father could down a bottle of whisky a day without slurring a syllable; my two sisters started on the gin or sherry before lunch, with or without company. I feared that slippery path and went round telling everyone that I was going to university. Telling everyone my plan meant I had to do it or lose too much face.

I went to Hornsby Technical College in 1973, sat for exams in English, History and General Studies and was accepted into Macquarie University as a mature age student. That whole first year my moods swung between wild elation that I was there, in a university, using my brain, and irrational fear that one day the gatekeeper, instead of smilingly waving me through, would say, 'Hey, what do think you're doing? You can't come in here.' It was scary, it was wonderful. I did not complete my BA until 1979, my studies being interrupted by two years in the UK (another company move), and a hysterectomy. During my last year, my daughter who was born in 1960 was in her first year and we had to sort out our relationship pretty quickly. Early on, she ran after me on campus, calling out 'Mum! Mum!' I did not turn round and when she caught up with me she asked why I had not answered. I told her that on campus I was just another student — not Brian's wife nor her mum — and she should call me by name. She did try, but occasionally she got it in reverse. That is how I came to have 'Mum' prefixed to my name. That was easiest.

I went on to do a graduate diploma in Library and Information Science at Ku-ring-gai College. That was nearly the course I did not finish. Brian had to pull the bedclothes off me some mornings and haul me out of bed. He must have got tired of giving me pep talks. It was not so much that the course was difficult but the workload was just too heavy. There was a high drop-out rate. When I got my first library job I found the course had been overloaded with theory — probably they thought we'd all go straight into library management — and I did not have an inkling about the smallest practicalities; even some of the terminology was unknown to me. Still, they must have got something right because I enjoyed a successful ten-year career in academic libraries before taking a redundancy during implementation of the Dawkins report.

Since I left work we have lived in London again, where I worked in the Citizens' Advice Bureau. Now I am a volunteer worker in the Australian Museum, involved with a women's action group, surrounded by my three children and four grandchildren, helping my husband with his consultancy business, creating a new home and enjoying a full social life with a wide circle of family and friends.

Sixty of those family and friends surround me now — one for each year of my life. They represent different interests and phases of my life but, apart from my cousin from New Zealand, they signify how indebted I am to Australia. My home is here where my heart is. It is time to make a public commitment.

My youngest son, six-foot three with shoulders to fill a doorway, looms beside me. 'What are you thinking about, Mum? You've been standing there for ages, lost in thought.' I turn to face him and say, 'I have decided to take out Australian citizenship.' I am confused by his reaction. His face expresses surprise, then relief. He folds me in his arms and, with my nose pressed into his chest, I hear him say: 'Oh, Mum, I'm so pleased. I've had the application forms for myself for ages but I was scared to tell you what I wanted to do because I thought you'd be unhappy about it.' I pull back, stand on tiptoe to kiss him: 'Well, we'd better go and tell your sister and see if she wants to join us.'

We link arms and march into the kitchen where my daughter is still working away, catering to the appetites of all the guests. She hears us out. 'Of course I'll do it. I always meant to; just never got round to it. Will you order application forms for me too?' We are joined in a three-way hug when Brian's voice interrupts us. It is time for the cake and toasts and 'Happy Birthday'. We follow him out to the verandah. I take up a full glass of champagne; I know what my toast will be.

Lottie Weiss in Bratislava, 17 March 1942

I have had two lives. My first life began in November 1923. That life ended in March 1942. That month I entered hell. I ceased to be a human being, a person with a name, with a future. (Instead I became a number —2065—one of the millions sentenced by Hitler to years of humiliation, deprivation and degradation.) For three long years, I barely survived physically. Mentally, I was already dead. In May 1945, I was born again. This time, though, I had to fend for myself all alone, for all traces of my family had been consumed by the gas chambers of Auschwitz. This is the story of my two lives.

Lottie Weiss in Auschwitz, 20 June 1942

MY TWO LIVES

Lottie Weiss

I was born in Bratislava, Czechoslovakia, on 28 November 1923. I was the third child and daughter in the family. I had two older sisters, Lilly and Erika, a younger sister, Renee, and two younger brothers, Karl Bernhard and Morris. My father was an accountant and a well-respected and loved man. My mother was caring and totally selfless, the most loving and kind person I have ever known and the perfect mother. We were brought up in a loving and caring atmosphere and were a very close family.

From 1939 onwards, the world situation was rapidly deteriorating and my country, Czechoslovakia, was changing drastically. On 14 March 1939 our part of the country became an independent state (Slovakia) and our head of state became Dr Josef Tiso, a Roman Catholic priest. The Hlinka Guard, the equivalent of the SS, carried out all duties in connection with the new anti-Jewish regulations and laws that came into effect daily. Jews were forbidden to go to school, all Jews had to hand in their furs and jewellery to the authorities, Jewish businesses were given Aryan managers who automatically became the owners, so the Jewish owners were forbidden to enter their own shops. Jews were ordered to live either in smaller centres outside Bratislava or were moved to Jewish quarters from the other parts of the city. And after 22 September 1941 all Jews were required to wear the Star of David on their left breast and communication with non-Jews was forbidden. It was a period of great activity for the Hlinka Guard: Jews were being insulted and beaten in the streets for no reason and the mood generally was very tense and unsafe. Our family life was totally disrupted. We were thrown out of our apartment in October 1941 and moved to the Jewish section of the city. Although there were eight members in our family we were allocated a small apartment consisting of one room and a kitchen.

Early in 1942 we heard rumours that all Jews would be resettled in Poland or Germany. It was said that young boys and girls would go first to prepare the work camps for their parents and younger siblings, who would follow soon after. When my parents heard this terrible news they wanted my two older sisters and me to leave Bratislava for Hungary, where the situation was less serious. Through a friend my father arranged for us to be taken illegally across the border by a guide for a certain sum of money; that was early in March 1942. However the authorities found out that some boys and girls had crossed the border illegally and announced that if young children were not found at home, their parents would be taken instead. When we heard this we did not want to leave, as our dear parents would have suffered the consequences.

One Sunday evening, 22 March 1942, three Hlinka Guards knocked on our door with the summons for the three eldest girls in the family, myself included, aged between eighteen and twenty-five years old. We were ordered to appear at seven the following morning in an old magazine factory called Patronka about six kilometres from Bratislava.

The last night in our parents' home was the worst of our lives. We stayed up all night to prepare our rucksacks, which my parents filled with food and clothing. We left home next morning at six: this was the last time we were ever together as a family and our 'Goodbyes' were final. This heartbreaking scene will remain in my memory forever.

When we arrived at seven, we saw many girls already assembled. We were ordered to leave all our belongings in the yard and then were taken, with about fifty-five others, to a room that was totally bare, except for a bucket to be used as a toilet. The degradation, the humiliation, the pain of sudden loss was unbearable and we cried bitterly. Being with my two sisters gave me some consolation, but the pain of leaving home was dreadful. Even today, after fifty-three years, I feel it.

We were given small quantities of food twice a day and allowed to use washing facilities only once a day under the supervision of the Hlinka Guard. After that we went back to our locked room. It was too cold at night for us to undress: we almost froze. We did not see anyone from the outside world, only the Hlinka Guard who shouted at us and ignored our questions. We remained there for five days.

On Friday 27 March 1942 all girls were ordered to assemble in the yard. We had to line up in fives and were counted numerous times. At around four in the afternoon, we were told to march towards the main railway station, accompanied by Hlinka Guards on foot and on horses. What a sad procession we were. Thrown out of our city, the place where our ancestors had lived for more than three hundred years, suddenly to become the enemy of the state and to be punished solely because we had been born Jewish.

We arrived at the railway station after a two-hour walk and were immediately told to climb into waiting cattle wagons. My two sisters and I held hands so as not to lose each other and we climbed into the wagon which already had a number of girls inside. We were herded in, sixty girls to a wagon, and the door was bolted behind us. We had two buckets for our toilet needs. We all huddled together as the train started to move, just to keep warm. A small opening at the top of the wagon was heavily barred; through it we could tell whether it was night or morning.

Early the following morning after about fourteen hours, we stopped. One girl lifted me up and I could see that we had stopped at a railway station called Zwardon on the border between Slovakia and Poland. There I saw the Hlinka Guards giving some documents to the SS guards; they were evidently taking charge of us. Some time elapsed before the train started moving again and we continued our sad journey for many hours. We stopped again, the bolted doors were unlocked and we were driven out by SS men with machine guns and Alsatian dogs. We did not move fast enough for them. They shouted at us 'Raus, raus, Jewish pigs, hurry up or you will be shot.'

Eventually we were all out and had to assemble there for our march to the concentration camp at Auschwitz. We did not know where we were, but as we marched towards the gate of the camp we saw the word *Gefahr* (danger) on the fences, indicating high-voltage wire. Above the gate were the words *Arbeit macht frei* (Work makes you free). We realised we had arrived at a concentration camp.

We were taken to a large hall inside the camp where we were registered and given numbers: mine was 2065. From that moment we ceased to have names and were known only by our numbers.

Then we were taken to another huge hall where we had to undress and were shaved by male prisoners. First they shaved our heads, then we had to stand on wooden stools and the male prisoners shaved our private parts, an experience I can never forget whose utter humiliation and shock are still with me. After this terrible experience, we had to go under a cold shower. We were then given Russian uniforms, which consisted of only trousers and a jacket: no underwear, vests, shoes or socks. Each girl was given a pair of wooden clogs which we were allowed to wear only at work. We were bitterly cold, tired and hungry.

My two sisters and I were taken, with about two hundred other girls, to Block 10 while other girls were taken to other blocks. There were one thousand girls in our transport. During the first night we had to lie on bare floors without blankets or food. We cried desperately the whole night.

The next morning, Sunday 29 March 1942, we had our first roll call on the camp street and afterwards had to assemble for work formation. My two sisters and I were ordered into a *Kommando* (work group) called *Strassenbau*. Our work consisted of digging ground, cutting trees and levelling the land in preparation for gardens. We worked in places that housed the SS officers and their families. It was hard and exhausting work we had not done before and all sixty girls in the *Kommando* suffered from hunger, thirst and cold. We were woken every morning at about three and had to hurry out onto the camp street for the dreaded roll call which lasted two to three hours.

Going to and from work we had to carry our wooden clogs and walk barefoot in all weather while we sang German marching songs. We were accompanied by SS men with machine guns and Alsatians. One morning a girl collapsed and my sisters went to help her. The SS men set a dog on them and it bit one of my sisters in the thigh. She was ordered back in line in spite of the fact that she was bleeding profusely. A minute later we heard a shot fired, killing the friend who had collapsed. We were ordered to carry her body to work and back, as the numbers of returning prisoners had to be the same as they had been that morning.

Each girl was allocated a piece of ground to dig. One day after I had finished my digging I wanted to help my sisters. An SS man came over and asked me what I was doing. When I told him he screamed at me, kicked me and said we were in a concentration camp, not a sanatorium. He told me he would report my misbehaviour to the camp authorities. A few weeks later, after roll call, I was told not to go to work the next morning, but to stay at the gate and wait for instructions. When I asked why, I was told I would be sent to the punishment camp for my misbehaviour.

We knew that no one ever came back from there. In the morning we cried bitterly as we kissed goodbye and my sisters went to work. I stayed at the gate and eventually more girls joined me until there were a number of us. A couple of hours later an SS officer called my number, 2065, and made me march to the men's camp to have my photo taken. We returned to the camp where the girls were still standing and waiting and soon after the gate opened and a black van arrived with two SS men, who ordered us into the van. One SS man stood by the van while the other counted. He got to twenty and pushed the last girl in. I was the twenty-first. He shouted at me and told me to get lost as he did not have enough room. I hesitated, but he told me again to 'get lost'. I ran quickly to my barracks and hid under the bunk because I was so frightened that he would come after me. But he didn't. When my sisters and I saw each other in the evening, we were so happy.

During the afternoon of that same day—20 June 1942—I heard some unusual noises on the camp street. At that time there were transports arriving daily from the occupied countries and I went to investigate. I noticed my cousin from Bratislava but she did not recognise me because of my shaven head and the Russian uniform I was wearing. I was, of course, much thinner than before. When I told her who I was, she started to cry and asked, 'In what hell have we landed?'

She told me that my parents, my younger sister and my two brothers were in the same transport as she was. At their arrival in Auschwitz, the SS put the newcomers into two groups. My cousin went to the right, as did my father and one brother; my mother and the two youngest in our family went to the left. She had no idea what it meant but I already knew that those on the left went to the gas chambers. After about two years in camp, I finally found out their fate: my father was beaten so badly he died after four days; one of my brothers lived for six weeks and then died of typhus. My mother, my youngest sister Renee and brother Morris went straight to the gas chambers.

I continued to work in the same *Kommando*. Our *Kapo* (forewoman) was Ulla, who had been a prisoner for many years in Ravensbruck. She was a German non-Jewish inmate who had been imprisoned because she was a prostitute. She and many other German non-Jewish prisoners were just as sadistic and vicious as the SS. When we marched out to work she asked me to march next to her in the first row with my sisters next to me. We were frightened of her because she constantly used her whip on us without any reason. One day she suddenly started to kick me and beat me with her whip and hands. After work I was aching so much that I could hardly walk.

The next morning at work assembly I asked her why she had beaten me. She said that a car with three SS officers had just passed our workplace and she wanted to show them how efficient she was; as I was closest I got the beating. The same day on our twenty-minute midday break she told us she had never seen a Jew in her life but had been brought up by her father to hate all Jews because they were not human. To our surprise she told us that we looked and talked exactly like her and she would try and treat us better from then on. Thereafter she became much more human.

Unfortunately, a short time later she fell ill with typhus and was taken to the hospital for non-Jewish prisoners. We were not allowed to visit her but my sisters and I, after returning from work and after roll call in the evening would wave to her from the window outside. She was always happy to see us and never forgot our interest in her. After her recovery she was our *Kapo* again until the beginning of September 1942 when she was made secretary to the camp commandant.

Our work became almost unbearable; with so little food, we collapsed like flies. Some girls in our group could not march out to work any more because they were so weak and ill. Many of them disappeared.

Since the end of May 1942 we had heard that girls who could not work or became ill would be gassed. The rumours became reality. There was a *Revier* (hospital) in camp where one was admitted only when one had a temperature of 41 degrees. We were frightened to go near it because it became obvious that most of the sick were taken by truck to the gas chambers.

Around June 1942, selections for the gas chamber started in the camp. These were repeated every four to six weeks. We had to stand on the camp street, totally naked, and pass two SS officers, keeping our hands and arms outstretched while they pointed to the right or left. My sisters and I used to pinch each other's cheeks to make us look healthier before we passed. The girls who were selected for the gas chambers were taken to trucks, shouting and screaming 'Let me live, let me live,' but then we heard shots fired and all was quiet.

One day at the end of July 1942, when we were at work digging soil and cutting trees, I got a terrible headache. On our way to camp, after work, I could not stand the pain any longer and told my sisters that I would go to the hospital after roll call. However, I collapsed and my two sisters and two other girls carried me to hospital in a blanket. I remained unconscious for three days and was put on the truck that took the very sick patients to the gas chambers. When I regained consciousness I was told by a nurse whose mother was a friend of my mother at home that she knelt down in front of the SS doctor and begged him to let me live because I was young, strong and a hard worker who had never missed a day of work. A miracle happened: he ordered someone to take me off the truck and sent a German nurse from the non-Jewish prisoners' hospital who gave me a lumbar puncture as she diagnosed meningitis. The pain of this injection brought me back to life and I started to scream with pain. The nurse shouted at me, 'If you scream, you will die. If you want to live, shut up.' I dug my fingers into the table and did not scream any more. I had no idea where I was, but was told to go back to my bunk. A Jewish nurse in this room helped me to a bunk and I immediately asked her about my two sisters. She told me that they came to see me every evening after work and roll call and promised to take me to the window so I could see them. When I saw them that evening, I collapsed again and had to be taken back to my bunk.

A few days later an SS woman came to the hospital and asked who among the patients could run. Although I could not even walk by myself yet, I said I could. This was the beginning of August 1942, and all prisoners who were staying in our part of the Auschwitz camp were moved to a different one a few kilometres away called Birkenau (Brzezinka). Of all the patients, only thirty girls told the SS woman that they could run, and they were taken to the other camp in Birkenau. I was among them; the rest of the patients went to the gas chambers.

It took me three days to find my sisters in this camp. There was chaos everywhere. There was no water or light, the streets were muddy, the huts were dirty and contained bunks which housed eight girls to one level. There were no toilets, only latrines; many girls were so weak that they fell in and drowned. The only water we drank was from puddles in the camp streets after rain.

I eventually found my sisters. They were in Block 27 and I moved in with them. I still felt ill and was very weak, but we were happy to be together again.

The day began at 3.30 in the dark, with the dreaded *Zahlappell* (roll call). The whole population of the camp fell into five lines, each group in front of its block, whatever the weather. The block seniors reported the number of prisoners to the *Rapportfuhrerin*. The roll call lasted for two or three hours, according to the will of the SS. We had to stand upright throughout, with those girls who had died in the meantime lying between us. After work we had another roll call and there we stood, exhausted and hungry, with not one word being spoken. These roll calls were the most-feared tortures. New transports were arriving daily from all occupied countries in Europe, the population was growing and the selections were carried out much more frequently. Of the thousand girls who came in my transport, by September 1942 only fifty were left. Most of the girls already knew that they had lost all their family. The miraculous thing was that they were still alive.

Lice crawled on our bodies and carried terrible diseases. A typhus epidemic broke out in the middle of September and both my sisters, Lilly and Erika, fell ill. They were delirious and too ill to stay in the barracks and were admitted to hospital. When I went to see them in the morning, before we marched out to work, they were barely alive. When I came to see them after work, I was not allowed in by the block senior. I begged her to let me see them, but she refused. I was desperate and tried the next day to see them again, but the same thing happened.

As I was standing in front of the hospital, desperate and not knowing what to do, I heard my name being called by two girls on the camp street. When I approached them, I recognised them as friends from my home town, carrying a stretcher with uniforms piled on it. I saw the number of one of my sisters on a uniform and found the uniform with the number of my other sister too. The girls told me that the uniforms came from Block 25. This was the collection or death block from which all prisoners went to the gas chambers or were brought there because they were already dead.

After learning of my sisters' death, I wanted to go to the electric fence and finish off my miserable life. There was no point in going on; I was alone in this world, desperate, hungry, ill and totally without hope. Suddenly I heard my name being called again and when I looked around, I saw Ulla, my former *Kapo*, now secretary to the camp commandant. She already knew my sisters had died and wanted to help me. When I told her that I had lost all hope and did not want to live any more, she took me to her barracks and gave me water and a piece of bread. She promised to help me find an indoor job where I would be kept away from the horrible climate and have a better chance to recover from my terrible loss. Ulla managed to get me into the 'Canada' *Kommando* where clothing was sorted from new inmates and sent to Germany for distribution to the German people.

In early December, we were lined up after work for roll call on the camp street and two SS women took out thirty girls at random from the assembled rows. I was among them. We were taken to the medical block on the other side and told to sit down in the anteroom when the first girl was called into the medical rooms. After at least twenty minutes the next girl was called in, and twenty minutes later the third girl was called in. None of the girls rejoined the group. After a while I became suspicious and asked the SS woman to allow me to relieve myself. She refused to let me go but I persevered and told her I had diarrhoea and could not wait any longer. She replied, 'Go, but come back immediately, otherwise we will drag you back.' I ran to the latrine and stayed there until dark, afraid to return to my barracks. The next day the girls told me they had been sterilised.

I worked in 'Canada' until the beginning of January 1943 and then through Ulla I got a job in an office. This was *Deutsche Erd und Steinwerke* (the German Mineral and Stone Works). Five other girls were accepted on the same day in the same office, each working in a different section. I was in accountancy, working with two civilians. As soon as we were accepted we were moved from Birkenau to Auschwitz and stayed in the *Stabsgebaude* (staff quarters). This job was the difference between life and death. We each had our own bunk and blanket, were able to shower daily and were given new uniforms, an apron and a white scarf to cover our shaven heads when we went to work; the office employees would not have worked with dirty people who would have brought lice and sicknesses to them. Although we still had very little food, the general conditions were so much better that we started to regain a little hope for our survival. After work and a short roll call (there were only about two hundred of us in this building), we were allowed to lie down, which meant we did not feel the hunger as much.

After having spent about two months in the office, I developed very bad boils and was running a high temperature. The SS woman *Kommandant* of the *Stabsgebaude* sent me to hospital. There I met a Polish doctor Janina Koszcziuszkowa, a political prisoner. She told me her husband was a judge in Krakow and she had an eight-year-old son. I asked her whether she wanted to send a message to them because the accountant in our office was Polish and went to Krakow often. She accepted gladly and I became the courier between her husband and son and our accountant. We stayed very good friends for many years until she died.

I continued to suffer from boils and from throat infections and I felt that my health had deteriorated considerably. I also suffered bad pains in my joints; at times I could not bend my fingers due to stiffness and pain. I was very fortunate that Dr Janina gave me a little medicine whenever she could.

In September 1944 we were moved to the new camp in Auschwitz, where we stayed until our evacuation on 18 January 1945. On that day all prisoners were moved into different camps towards the west. The six girls who worked in the office were first taken to Gross-Rosen then to Neu-Rohlau then to Flossenburg, then to Hainichen and finally to Theresienstadt, where we arrived on 21 April 1945. Rumours were spreading that the camp was mined and would be blown up. However we were liberated by Russian troops on the night of 8 and 9 May 1945.

The unbelievable had happened. I ran out on the street, saw my first Russian soldier and kissed his hands and said, 'Thank you,' a thousand times. We were deliriously happy and could not believe that we were free again – after thirty-eight months of pain, misery, hopelessness, and the loss of my beloved family. But what now? Where could we go?

Three days later, volunteers with trucks took all those who wanted to leave to Prague. The six of us accepted with deep gratitude and we were soon on our way to Prague and to our long-awaited freedom. We spent the night at the Jewish community office and in the morning were taken to the office of the Joint Distribution Committee where we were given the address of a hotel in Prague whose owner took as guests people returning from the concentration camps. We stayed there a few days but I wanted to return to Bratislava. As no passenger trains were going yet, we were put in open coal wagons with many other people.

After travelling for three days I arrived in Bratislava on Saturday 19 May 1945. It was a very strange feeling to arrive home and I could not believe it was really happening. It was 8.30 pm when I arrived at the railway station and signs stated that there was a curfew after 9 pm. I did not know where to go or what to do. I had no idea whether any of my relatives had survived, whether there was anyone in the city who remembered me.

I remembered the Maraky family, non-Jewish friends of my parents and made my way towards their apartment. I rang the bell downstairs and looked up towards the fourth floor. The son of my friends came out on the balcony and asked who it was. When I said who I was, he shouted: 'Are you alone? Where are Lilly, Erika and the rest of the family?' He came downstairs and when he saw me, he took me in his arms and started to cry. He was still crying when we arrived on the fourth floor.

His sister Magda and his father were at home but his mother was visiting relatives out of town. They made me most welcome and asked me whether I wanted to eat, but I could not eat and all I wanted was a cup of coffee. They asked me a million questions, but I was too emotional and upset to answer some of them. I could not believe that I was back, a free person. At about three o'clock in the morning I could no longer stay awake and Magda gave me her bed to sleep in. What luxury, what bliss, to be in a proper clean bed with an eiderdown and feather pillow! I asked Mr Maraky to wake me at eight because I wanted to go to the Joint Distribution Office to find out about people who were registered there after returning from the war. He tried to wake me but I was sleeping so heavily that he only succeeded at eleven. I hurriedly had a cup of coffee and left.

At the Joint Office I found out that my uncle and aunt had come back to Bratislava two days before and I went to see them. They were both at home when I arrived and at first glance they did not recognise me. They asked me where my parents, sisters and brothers were and I told them they had all perished in the gas chambers of Auschwitz. My aunt winked at my uncle; she could not believe what I had just said and thought I was mad. I was deeply hurt and I did not say anything more. I stayed with them until 1947 and never spoke to them about my experiences again. (When I look back I am sorry that I could not talk to them about Auschwitz; I now realise that ordinary people would have found what happened to us completely incredible.)

I went back to the Marakys and told them about moving to my uncle's house; they insisted I should stay with them longer and I stayed another night. I will never forget their wonderful welcome when I arrived from hell. I was twenty-one years old, weighed less than five stone and was broken in body and spirit.

My first days of freedom were wonderful. I went on the street without a guard and when I looked behind me, there was no SS man with a machine gun nor was there an Alsatian dog just waiting for his bait. One of my girl-friends, Illi, who worked with me at the office in Auschwitz, was living not far from me. I felt happiest when I was with her; we shared our experiences and no one who had not gone through this hell could understand our feelings. (Illi met a young man in the Joint Office soon after her return and later he became her husband.) People who were not in camp looked at us in astonishment, surprised that anybody at all came back. We almost had to apologise for surviving. Statistics show that 85,000 Jews from Slovakia were deported in 1942 to various extermination camps in Poland and a pitiful 236 of us returned. Those few only survived because they worked in offices, laundries, sewing rooms or kitchens.

A few weeks after my return, the reaction started. There was no time when I did not think of my beloved family, and I started to ask: 'Why am I here and you are not? What have I done to deserve a return from hell? You were condemned to death and I was condemned to life. Wherever I go, I remember you – always. How will I continue with my life? No one would have missed me if I had not returned. I do not belong to anybody, nobody belongs to me.'

One morning I could not get up, feeling totally depressed and unable to think. My aunt called a doctor who diagnosed a nervous breakdown and ordered full rest and regular food. I was confined to bed for about three weeks and slowly regained my health. As soon as the doctor allowed me, I looked for a job and was accepted as a typist clerk in a law office. Although I liked my job, I was restless and unhappy and it troubled me greatly that I had lost faith in God.

I went to see a rabbi to ask his explanation for this unbelievable tragedy which tortured me night and day. At night I heard the screams of the children as they were thrown into the fire and I smelled burning human flesh. I asked the rabbi, 'How could it have happened?' He was very understanding, listening to me patiently without saying one word. Then after a while he told me, 'There is no answer, my child, and I cannot give you an explanation. I can, however, tell you that God did not take a revolver and shoot anyone. God did not build the gas chambers. God has given the human being the wisdom to differentiate between good and evil and every human being decides what to choose.' Although he did not convince me I felt a bit happier. Three months later I saw another rabbi, whose explanations were the same and I saw that it was up to me to decide what to do. Slowly I regained my faith in God, as I could not live without believing in God and humanity.

About a year after the war, my future husband asked me for a date and I liked being in his company. We were happy when we were together and we were married in 1947. My husband was also a survivor, which was very important to me. He was twenty years older than me and I felt he could replace some of my lost loved ones with his kindness and understanding. He and his brother were the only surviving members of his big family. His brother was married in 1946 to a girl whose brothers had migrated to New Zealand in 1939. The brothers sent them a permit and they left early in 1948. When they arrived in New Zealand they sent us a permit and we arrived in Wellington on 15 August 1949. We were accepted with great love and understanding by our new family and our new life started to give us back some happiness. The greatest joy for us was when our first son, John Michael, was born on 25 August 1951 and when our second son, Gary Hilton, was born on 25 May 1953.

My husband, Alfred (Ali), unfortunately passed away in June 1982, and our sons and daughters-in-law moved to Sydney. I followed soon after. After the initial settling-in period, I am very fortunate to live in this beautiful city and be very close to my beloved family. I am blessed with four grandsons and two granddaughters and I see them very often. I have a full-time position as a bookkeeper and on Sundays I do volunteer work in the Sydney Jewish Museum, which I find most fulfilling and gratifying.

I am most grateful that God gave me back my life, as I am rewarded every moment.

SISTER

Gabrielle Bates

I first turned the pages of Fru Fru's visual diary seven years ago. It's a strange arrangement we keep, but she thinks it's healthy for her. Fru believes that if she can relinquish the preciousness of her visual diaries, she will begin each year with a fresh slate. She refuses to be bound by sentimentality. The knowledge that her past ideas are festering and smouldering and imploding far out of her reach helps her to grow and renew herself yearly. She sends her diaries, these secret, private moments, to me, her sister — thousands of miles away — from Sydney to America.

Of course, I don't mind receiving these paper-bound morsels. But it's hard to understand why she should want to give them up so readily. If I were Fru I would hold onto them for dear life; I would etch out the threads of continuity within my project, watching my creativity ripen.

I keep the diaries in secret guilt, fearful that I covet small mysteries, for that is exactly the power they have. I am frightened that one day she will want them back. I am frightened she may destroy them altogether.

They are not so old, but already they release that familiar scent of ageing texts, reminiscent of our mother's photograph albums. This first diary is falling to pieces. It is a hotchpotch of magazine and postcard images, interspersed with hand-sketched experiments and nervous poetry. It is naive and shy. She is playing and testing herself. Here is a montage of abject poverty and over the page is an illustration of a dead man lying face down in a graveyard. A photograph of herself dressed up as her grandmother, next to an exploding pineapple! Fru Fru is making jokes, discovering her subconscious, wondering about the injustices of the world.

Fru Fru

I am putting together some images on black canvas grounds. They are rendered in white over black paint, derived from small photos of my face. I begin to smudge and blend the renderings so any detail dissolves and becomes ghosted. They appear fleeting, like a memory or a glimpse, open to interpretation and, more appropriately, misinterpretation. Slippage.

I want to suggest shifting meaning, something transient and unfixed. I want to grasp a lost expression or a moment indefinable.

These images have a deathly quality, lost spectres whose uncertain representation remains.

I don't suppose I know who I am any more.

But I had stopped screaming. My mind was somewhere up with the stars that hung like periwinkles on a giant black wave-swept platform. My leg was up there too, hanging down in the moonlight, pale and limp. I wondered whether I would live or die, and if I lived ... perhaps I would have to spend endless hours on a psychiatrist's couch. Banal thoughts reminiscent of a *Cosmo* magazine. Thoughts slipped to blue mangoes and yellow-pages textbooks, Our Lady of the Sacred Heart and finally to my mother.

I wanted to think about anything except where I was.

To light and extinguish (my) desires.
To contain and negate.
To bottle and preserve.
Does the mute poet wish to entrap the flame?
Or is she the one trapped in the network,
Preserved like a specimen in a bottle?

The Author

A good question.

In fact, to uncover any rationale behind these nonsensical, fragmented babblings, you and I must become tourists and travel into the past. We must take the AutoFrag Bus No. 22 en route to about six years ago and alight in the distant interior.

Can you see her?

There she is. The dance on the hill is long over. Fru Fru is upset at being stood up by a friend who was to walk her back to the hotel. It is now dark early morning, thankfully cooler and more tolerable than the dry desert heat of the day. A scrub-scented breeze rises over the escarpment and travels along the road with her. There are other smaller groups of young people on the road also, but she keeps away from them out of shyness. Secretly, though, she wishes for company. She passes two men sitting on a motorcycle by the side of the road and feels stupidly flattered when they shine their headlight on her, so her entire form throws a huge silhouette up onto the hillside. She is a romantic, and in her thin dress her shadow could be mistaken for Andromeda, chained and waiting for her perilous meeting with the sea monster. She chuckles to herself at the thought then remembers her disappointment.

The road begins its decline to the flat, silent plain, and she has gone only minutes further when she hears the motorcycle rumble up behind her. She moves to the side of the road to allow it to pass but the men, doubling, pull over and begin to speak to her.

They are not from around these parts. They are foreigners. Strong accents.

She can be amiable when necessary and has learnt from travelling that a smile is the best international language.

'Hellooooo, how are you?'

'Hi.'

She continues to walk, and thinks she recognises one of the men as another hotel guest, but isn't certain. The men allow the bike to amble up close and ride alongside her at walking pace.

'Wanna ride on my bike?' asks the young man, and she sees the opportunity of getting back to the hotel quickly. She has convinced herself that the older man is from her hotel.

'I need a lift to the hotel down the road,' she offers, and is surprised at the alacrity with which the younger man jumps off and motions her to climb aboard. The men laugh and she straddles the seat. It is dangerously amusing to think of three people on a bike together, appealing to Fru Fru's warped sense of humour. The man on the road climbs up behind her and puts his hands on her hips, the motor revs and the bike slowly pulls away from the side of the road.

The road is deliciously curly, a rainbow serpent unfolding before them. The dark wind encircles her ears and she closes her eyes, smiling now, as she travels in silence down, down on the back of Pegasus, snorting and galloping on his flight of deliverance.

But something is wrong. The road turns left to travel alongside the dry river bed and she knows the bike must turn right to get to the hotel. The man in front does not seem to acknowledge her insistence the hotel is in the other direction. She leans forward and grabs the handbrake, squeezing it hard so the bike comes to a total standstill.

'Take me to my hotel,' she demands through clenched teeth, furious that all of a sudden the men can no longer speak English.

The man behind grasps her arms tightly and the driver prises her fingers from the handlebar. The bike begins to move again. She screams, loud, damned if she is going to allow the bloody bike to move another inch. If she has to, she will walk to the hotel from this stupid, abandoned place they have brought her to.

The bike has moved at least ten feet further when she puts full-struggle-and-fall-off into operation. She kicks, squirms and pushes so hard that the man behind is forced bit by bit off the back of the bike. He grips on desperately with his thighs, using Fru Fru as an anchor, but she persists and wriggles frantically. The bike sways to and fro. Finally, still restraining her, the man behind is ripped off the back of the bike and she lands heavily on top of him, hoping to God she has winded him properly.

The bike scrapes heavily along the empty dirt road to a thumping halt and the other man is thrown into a small ditch.

The only problem is that Fru Fru's leg is still stuck behind the exhaust pipe and when the motorcycle comes to its halt, the tibia and fibula bones snap like tree twigs and she realises, *Oh fuck, I've broken my leg.* Pegasus is down. The sea monster, the Bungalunga, the boogie man has arrived.

She screams and cries and pleads with them to take her to a hospital. The men, having recovered easily, begin to taunt her, touching her legs, her shoulders, cooing softly as they poke her broken leg. She drags herself away from them, crying, choking on the dust. She slides into the ditch. The men are amused in the same way children enjoy pulling wings off cicadas. They pull off her underpants and she sobs into subservience, unable to escape, in too much pain to fight.

Suddenly Fru Fru McKenzie has been thrust into a hostile
environment; the place she had once known as home. Her
security has been taken away, her trust of the world
betrayed. Her mind reels with questions. She wants to
know who she is. Her sense of self, that familiar old friend
on whom she had come to rely, has departed for the stars
on the waveswept platform.

Fru Fru's friends are terrified by the enormity of the
rape. They refuse to address it except in a sensational manner. Her young friends have no way of dealing with distress and crisis. The absence of war from Australia in the
last fifteen years and the security derived from US hyper-
reality makes Fru Fru's situation unnerving and horrific
for them. Not because of the rape itself nor the confronta-
tion of its possibility, but the undiscussed realisation they
have no skills to offer her in the way of consolation or
healing.

They run from Fru Fru's position as victim, try to dis-
tract her from it. They will not hear of it, they will not
grieve for her. They will turn the incident into delicious
gossip or taboo family shame.

She feels afraid. When she speaks of her fear, that shaking horror that makes her agoraphobic and suspicious of
strangers, they stroke her shoulders and say: 'Don't worry,
there's nothing to be frightened of.'

But there is plenty to be worried about. She is terrified.
She can't watch the news on television at night because it
is so violent. She can't read books because everything
seems to allude to power imbalance and victimisation,
constantly reminding her of the rape. People want her to
snap out of it, but she just wants to hide and wallow.

Then there is a change.

Someone suggests to her that revenge is an excellent
solution. Fru Fru knows she does not want violence or ret-
ribution, but she does want a solution to all this fuss. And
it is fuss. The friends come with flowers and chocolates to

look at her, pat her, tell her that if there's anything she needs ...

The uncertainty about how she should deal with the predicament helps her decide to turn her experience into something positive. After all, she thinks she is a creative being. She believes that if she can use the rape as a means for growth and celebration in herself, it can no longer have power over her. It will dissolve under the pressure of her joy that it happened. Fru Fru will be grateful to her rapists for their contribution to her destiny.

Fru Fru escapes into positivism and catharsis. And this is where she first picks up the paintbrush seriously, without any intention of putting it down again.

Sister

This next book demonstrates Fru's experimentation with colour, texture and design. Ever since she was a child she has had a talent for colour, she dabbles in putting together the most unusual hues. Her sketching becomes more diligent here, she is playing with marks and overlaying. There is a greater awareness of content in her choice of imagery, too. Questions of the body and primitivism appear, look at this black and white photograph of a man with a Papua New Guinea mask for a head. It's unsettling because the man is white. He doesn't belong with that mask, does he?

We always knew she'd be an artist, she's so much more sensitive than the rest of us. Fru was always sketching something or other, putting together little books, making up stories and acting them out. It's such a shame that it took that awful thing in the desert to bring her into a greater self-awareness.

Fru Fru

What was that space in me that the act of creation seemed to fill?

I was driven to make images. I liked being identified as an exotic imitator and society conjurer. The artist. It appealed to my vanity because an artist sometimes has secrets. And there is power in mystery.

I could not say my ability to paint came from a divine source. I do not possess the 'gift of genius' (I am a woman after all ...). What basic 'lack' did this useless cultural production of mine satisfy?

Yes. I wanted to do something positive for myself. I wanted a secret goal. I believed it was only a matter of time before I could conquer fear itself.

Perhaps I was even searching for passion, the very thing a rape victim is denied.

Ultimately I gave myself over to my own desire. I had previously spent most of my time fulfilling the desires of others, years of insecurity.

Now it was my turn to enjoy myself.

The Author

The people do not approve of her tactic. They think she should suffer appropriately a little more. They cannot believe it when she tells them she has resumed sexual relations. They assume that because she was not a virgin before it happened, the experience of the rape could not have been as traumatic as they suspected.

It does not occur to them there may be a blockage. Or a denial. And even if this were true, such a revelation would not stop Fru Fru from packing her trunk and going interstate. People cannot understand why she should want to leave them. Why should she want to be alone? She was filled with fear only a week ago, terrified to leave the house.

They are scandalised when she begins to send them photos of her first attempts at painting. The images celebrate horror-stricken screaming women, pain and terror.

This scandal is both delightful (because, they feel, it is predictable) and worrisome (maybe she is losing her mind). Ripples of concern stretch out to her but she writes back to them from her place of respite in Victoria with an unnervingly cheery voice.

Fru Fru wants them to think she is all right.

She wants them to drop her subject and get over it. On the other hand, however, she has no intention of doing such a thing. She intends to exploit it.

In less than a year Fru Fru's approach to her environment changes dramatically.

This quiet country, once warm and comfortable as it hid beneath the sheltering skirts of English imperialism and European tastes, becomes threatening and dangerous.

On returning home from Victoria she is disturbed by the tensions brewing in her neighbourhood. People have TV accents and wear TV clothes. Local crime is rated by its entertainment value. She reminisces about the times when she could eat an ice cream for its taste and not its logo or walk the cosy middle Australian streets at night unprotected.

Rather than accepting everything she is told, rather than swallowing every truth she is handed, Fru Fru begins to ask questions. Fru Fru learns the art of challenge, critical of the world around her as well as the person within.

Fru Fru

Dear (colleague),

Do you remember when we left that movie we had a feeling of depression and shock? And yesterday I walked out of S. in the first hour. I think I may be a hypocrite. You see, I approached these films from what I think may be conflicting points of view, that is, female, middle-class, Australian, rape victim ... then of course, on the other hand, artist (simplified terms of self definition). I'm extremely confused about what stand I should take in reaction to these films, *S.* in particular.

I was horrified by *S.* Yet I went home and masturbated. You may say I should just go with what was my first, knee-jerk reaction — but this, I feel, is behaviour that has been learned: I think society has told me to be horrified or at least to react in a horrified manner, and therefore I must censor the event from my personal experience. But from an artistic point of view I felt a fascination, an enjoyment at the spectacle, the voyeurism itself, divorced from my shocked, structured, rape victim self. Likewise, there was an odd pleasure in identifying with the tortured characters. Perhaps the artist and the victim are not so separate after all.

Love, Fru Fru

Here is Fru Fru's breakthrough. While baring her private moments of thought on thin slips of paper to close friends, she discovers her sensual self, and although frightened, she is exploring it through confused letters, private performance and paintings in wax.

The canvases, six feet by four feet, have a phenomenal impact on her life. She is searching for the repressed spaces of sensuality lying within the institution, she is pointing her finger at the constructed self and alluding to censorship.

In creating these works, she strangely feels fear again for the first time since her rape. Something is touching her beyond her consent, but this time she cannot see the hands.

Sister

The third book is more aesthetically refined. It is slick. Glossy. Its paper sticks together because the paint and collage are so thick. Smell it, it reminds me of thinners and enamels.

I think Fru might be wrestling with her first taste of post-modernity but she doesn't seem quite ready to relinquish her enjoyment of modernist mysteries. And she is constantly looking outside herself for answers.

Without warning, however, the writings and pictures shift. There are images of Fru Fru dressed up in different guises: a vampish seductress, a coy wallflower, a bound white victim. There is a sexy, self-conscious girlishness that has been absent from her other books. The images make me feel nervous. There are private writings about wet dreams and closet lesbianism. The photos and texts become sketchy and messy, no longer so concerned with design or beauty. They are scratchy, crude. Look, here is the image of the bandaged woman with five cigars stuffed in her mouth, next to the woman having her nipples squeezed. She is tied up in octopus straps.

Unlike these new approaches in the visual diaries, Fru's paintings are highly detailed (I've seen them in photos). First she lays down ripped pieces of pornographic material in a collage on the canvas. Next she layers the collage with pornographic images of women in subservient positions. Over this is stencilled hot wax into shapes that symbolise church windows so the pornographic women peek through. The wax, its fumes smelly and overpowering, is poured or flicked: thick and luscious and dribbling. When dry it looks like semen. Finally, Fru paints in oils an image of our parents getting married and surrounds it with pink love hearts and baby-blue sky.

The Author

A painting in the newspaper captures Fru Fru's attention: two women picking flowers in a serene landscape. It occurs to her that the black-and-white newspaper reproduction does not do the image any justice, so she reads on.

The painter is a murderer. He has committed multiple

sex crimes and now, in gaol, he paints to whittle away his exile. He paints pictures of animals, landscapes, sometimes he even copies photographs of dead children for their grieving parents. The painting in question has been rejected by an auctioneering house, whose staff feel the image exemplifies the painter's fantasies of his previous crimes committed more than thirty years ago. Thus the piece has been refused auction on moral grounds.

What does Fru Fru do?

Should she cheer on the censors, congratulating them for silencing another evil force in society? Should she admonish them for placing too much emphasis on what could really be described as only a kitsch chocolate-box picture?

Fru Fru is alarmed. Fru Fru is disappointed. Fru Fru is incensed.

She writes.

Dear (murderer),

I firmly believe that others should not have the right to use their power in determining whether an individual's creative intentions are right or wrong.

The context or circumstances of your position should not even be entered into when it comes to questioning the integrity of your creative product, unless of course you feel it is relevant to the artwork. Especially in a field as enriching as painting.

If your painting were put to auction anonymously I cannot imagine anyone having major moral problems with the work. However, given the nature of your history, people have chosen to discriminate against you. They choose to punish you for expressing yourself in a non-violent way. This is outrageously unfair. It is a moral judgment on art. It is truth assumed through pure illusion. Do these people really think that an evil aura can lurk in the two-dimensional veneer of a painted surface?

It appears quite ironic to me — the problem seems to lie more in their minds rather than in any message this painting may convey.

Nevertheless, I ask this question: Why should people be unable to express their fantasy/vision/desire/fetish/sense of irony or humour/religious or spiritual belief in a productive way? Why do people in powerful positions believe they can even deny us our dreams?

Wouldn't it be nice to think that in these times we may be able to retain some convoluted sense of freedom of expression?

Regards,
Fru Fru McKenzie

Fru Fru

When I wrote that letter I wanted to transcend, for it was truly time.

To forgive.

To know myself.

Identity is forged from pain. To write such a letter was profoundly painful, because it made me realise there is no such thing as freedom. It seemed so ironic to write to someone in gaol about such an idea. Oh, but how appropriate?

This body, this mind, this spirit: they are all products of violence and struggle. Oh melodrama, so theatrical and delicious!

Call me a *femme fatale* if you like. I will thank you kindly, for I am Australia herself.

Once upon a time I was classical. I was Andromeda. A victim defined by male mythologies.

Now I am a victim defined by me, I, us. Carved by my own hand. A victim of myself.

Does it come from my convict heritage (that unspoken past that is only between these lines) ... all that chipping and quarrying at Argyle Place? Port Arthur? I wonder ...

These skirts and frills and chains and horror and sweat and toil, God, they make me what I am. How can I not like that? How can I not find this pleasurable?

I can take great pride in being such a ... a ... a Fru Fru.

Fru Fru's Dream

In the dream we are in that bush place I know very well, but have not yet been to (or maybe I have been, but don't remember). My older sister is driving her friend and me to the residence of an old man for whom she occasionally does housekeeping. We find no one home in his pole shack at the top of the gorge. My sister has the front-door key, so we go in and look at the old man's possessions.

I become tired so my sister suggests I lie down (on the old man's bed) while she shows something in the bush to our friend. I express my nervousness about the old man returning, but my sister says, 'It's all right, I won't be long.'

When I finally wake, I feel angry. The hours have passed but there is no sign of my sister. The day is almost over. I am terrified our trespassing will be discovered.

Sure enough, a car pulls up and out pops the old man.

I explain who I am but the old man doesn't appear terribly worried that a stranger is sitting in his house. 'Oh yes,' he says, 'you're the artist.' I presume my sister has told him about me, but I am still livid at her for putting me in this situation.

Then the old man says, 'Follow me.' I trust him. We walk into the bush to an enormous building, as big as a cathedral, but with frontier-type architecture. Inside, it is overgrown with two-metre-high weeds, and there are agapanthus. On the vast walls are grand paintings as immense as rock faces. These enormous paintings depict historical events, they are landscapes, abstracts, post-modern. There are even images that are cinematic and moving.

Majestic music is softly piped throughout the weedy, cavernous room. The pathways are thoroughly concealed with wild plant life, but are also overrun with elfin creatures tending to the artworks.

I feel overwhelmed and moved to cry at this spectacle, ambiguously eased by the familiarity of this unfamiliar place in my head. I want to run and embrace every last image in the room, welling with unprecedented, sappy emotion. And as I wake my pillow is covered with tears.

OPAL FEVER OR TOTAL INSANITY

Karen Heap

In the Beginning

It's 1984 and I'm a single, hopefully sane, thirty-four-year-old woman with two spoilt dogs. I've lived in the city all my life, and yet for some peculiar reason, for as long as I can remember I've always wanted to go to the opal fields.

I have no idea why. Maybe I saw something on TV when I was a kid and liked what I saw. Anyway, now I have the opportunity I've loaded my car to the hilt, squeezed my two dogs and myself into my faithful old Gemini sedan and here I am, heading off into the middle of nowhere, leaving my long-suffering family and friends behind. Mum's sure I take after Dad's side of the family. My sisters think I might have been adopted.

Too late now, can't turn back. I've left my job and sold my little house. Bought my very own opal mining claim and one-room camp, complete with dirt floor, window flaps and pit toilet. One of the best outside loos on the field, so I was told.

Mining out here on this isolated field is not overly difficult. It's not like the Ridge (Lightning Ridge) where they have to take their opal dirt to the puddling tanks, which would be too difficult for me to handle alone.

That's why I ended up out here in this wilderness. The mining procedure is easier. There is no water out here to puddle anything. It's all dry mining. There are no services either; no electricity, no sewerage, no phones, no water, no roads, no shops. Nothing. Zilch. Zero.

What is out here is a very rare breed of men, almost extinct I'd say, but not quite. Willing to fight the elements and take a chance. Hoping to find the strike that will set them up for life. I've now invaded their stronghold and life will never be the same again.

I hope I survive this outback adventure, though being an A1 coward when it comes to roughing it and freaking out at all spiders and bugs, I'm not so sure. Ah well, one can only try. I plan to stay for a year; that should give me plenty of time to strike it rich or die trying.

Why shouldn't I have a go? Just because I'm a woman shouldn't make any difference at all. I don't know, though; maybe I am going mad or just having an early menopause.

The Great Flood

When I first arrived on the field the mines were just recovering from a major flood. The flat area leading into the field is called Rotten Plain. It was flooded for months with fish trapped from the overflow of the Narran River.

The miners built a high narrow strip of dirt running right through the middle of this plain, our only way in and out of the field. It was like the parting of the Red Sea. I was scared witless the whole lot was going to collapse and I'd be swallowed up by it all, just like the Egyptians. Nothing but water for miles and miles.

It was an awesome sight. Pelicans were everywhere, catching fish, and I thought that was a good idea. I could go down every day and catch some fresh fish for tea. I soon discovered, like the Europeans, that carp is quite a delicacy if cooked properly and eaten with the fingers to remove the hundreds of bones.

In the end as the plain gradually dried up I just caught the fish by hand and carted them home by the bucketful. But the novelty soon wore off when the fish started dying; the stench was unbelievable. No wonder they called it Rotten Plain. Just as well it wasn't an everyday occurrence or all the miners would be wearing gas masks.

The Brown-streaked Toffee

I settled into my little one-room camp with gusto. It had been nicknamed the Honeymoon Cottage; all previous owners had been newlyweds, apparently. I was the first single person in the camp to break the spell.

It was not all plain sailing, though. My thousand-gallon water tank was contaminated with gumnuts and leaves so the water was brown and undrinkable. I ended up having to cart twenty-litre drums of water from the tanks of the miners' little social club, to get me by until I could clean out my tank and secure a safe water supply.

I was just using the tank water for washing and showering until my clothes and I started turning brown. This water was better than any dye. I really didn't mind my hair going brown and the grey hairs disappearing, but I was now in dire straits as I had to dispose of the water completely. I didn't like looking like a brown-streaked toffee and my clothes looked awful. I was breaking my back as I carted even more water from the club, using it very sparingly until the rain came to fill my tank again.

I didn't have long to wait. In my second week the rain clouds started building up. Everyone started to batten down the hatches. The wind was ferocious and I was told that they suffer some really bad storms. My neighbours lost their roof and were nearly flooded out in the last big storm, which was like a mini-tornado. Half the miners lost their roofs.

No one mines when the weather is like this; it's too dangerous. They all hibernate and prepare for the worst. The mines take a long time to dry out also after a storm, even when the water is pumped out of them. My mine still had a damp floor, but I was hopeful the dogs and I would survive the expected onslaught.

About midnight one night, crackling lightning and roaring thunder woke me up, startled. I raced outside to close my window flaps so my dirt floor and carpet would not get wet. I had only sheets of iron for windows, with flaps secured by wire on the wall.

I had to smile; everyone else on the field was out with their torches making last-minute adjustments. When everything seemed to be secure we all gathered in a large group in our night attire discussing the weather, speculating whether it would rain.

I thought my family wouldn't believe this. Here I was in the middle of the night, talking about the weather. We all chatted for about half an hour then everyone gradually drifted off to their own camps to await the storm.

I was amazed at the importance of the weather out here; I'd never bothered watching the forecast in the city as it really didn't affect me greatly. Now I was discussing the weather at midnight and hoping I wouldn't lose my roof.

It was a false alarm that time; there are a lot, and the rain clouds passed us by. I was relieved in a way as I was still trying to get my camp organised. The ants were on the rampage, along my back inside wall and the door. There seemed to be millions of them, quite savage and with a nasty bite. They were horrible creatures and their aggressiveness was a definite sign of rain, or so the old timers told me.

Insect spray seems to be useless against them too. One of the miners gave me some kerosene to douse them with, which stopped them for the moment. I kept thinking of Them, a horror movie about ants, with visions of being eaten alive by the savage little creatures. Even the dogs avoided them.

I organised with Pommie Bill, one of the miners, to build up a thick layer of opal dirt all around the camp with his front-end loader, to try and stop my camp from flooding and to cover up all the gross burrs. I also asked him to put a nice high foundation at the back of the camp for a shed to be built.

My neighbour also had a wall of opal dirt put around his camp to stop it flooding; I hoped it would protect my camp as I was down the slope from him. Nothing was wasted out there, I discovered, not even the dirt.

Then I had to buy some sheets of iron for the shed so I would have somewhere to put the generator when I bought one. It took me a while to get organised as everything moved so slowly out there. Of course I was a million miles away from town, but I was sure I'd adjust.

Neighbours

Everyone was so kind and helpful to me from the moment I arrived on the field, offering me all sorts of advice and information as well as water, which was as scarce as hens' teeth out there. Old Tom even brought me over a sulphur potion for my dog Pinky, a fox-terrier cross that suffered all sorts of allergies. The club president was also called Pinky, but I didn't think he was allergic to anything.

Old Tom's bush remedy worked wonders and Pinky (the dog) was soon free of her skin complaints. After years of vets' visits it took a simple potion to cure her.

Another neighbour said I could use a lead off his generator when it was working until I could find a suitable generator. I was delighted as I was still trying to get used to silence and candlelight; being able to listen to the radio and run a light was wonderful.

There was one minor problem, however; I had no warning when the neighbour intended to turn off the generator.

It was most unpleasant when everything went black and I was in the middle of sewing something and making repairs. I ended up fumbling around in the dark, trying to light the candles. I learned to carry a candle and matches with me to save any future mishaps.

This roughing it, I discovered, was not all it was cracked up to be: sweeping out my camp with a straw broom, handwashing everything, washing up in a bowl were all new experiences I can tell you. I couldn't keep any food out there either; even the eggs went off in the heat. I decided to try and get some live chooks in for food.

I didn't even bother wearing my digital watch any more; it just went haywire from the heat. But no one seemed really to worry about the time out there, everyone was very laid back and relaxed.

I was learning all sorts of useful things, such as how to have a sponge bath out of a bucket of water. How to use a very practical gadget that pumped up my tyres from the car battery. How to tell the pressure of tyres. Such useful information; just what I'd always wanted to know.

Much Ado about Nothing

I finally bought myself a jackhammer, lights, leads and a Honda 2 kVA generator to give me about 2,000 watts of electricity. Enough power to run a hoist when I bought one and my jackhammer. Of course I tried out the generator before I purchased it, as all the men said I wouldn't be able to start a generator. It was no different to starting a lawnmower so I didn't know what all the fuss was about.

A few of the women on the field then started to operate their generators instead of having to wait until their husbands came home to start them. I'm amazed that some people don't give things a try before they say, 'I can't do it, it's too hard.' I wouldn't have been there at all if I'd listened to everyone's negative advice.

Mr Fixit

One of my neighbours, Big Joe, offered to take me down his mine to show me how it all worked. There I was, all keen and ready to go, when he dropped an oil bomb down the shaft to get rid of the mosquitoes. 'Only take a minute,' he said. He must have overloaded his little bomb; we waited half an hour for the smell of burning oil and smoke to leave the mine.

All set again, we climbed down his safety ladder. No one used the main ladder with the hoist connected in case it was accidentally turned on and the hoist bucket came crashing down. It could have killed someone or injured them severely. I was very impressed to think that Big Joe was so safety-conscious.

I happily climbed down the mine shaft to be met by the foul-smelling acrid smoke of the oil bomb, which nearly choked me to death. Persevering, I started to mine, following his instructions, when a huge boulder fell on my foot and nearly broke my toe. I started to jump around in agony as Big Joe looked on quite amused. Trying not to be a wimp, I recovered quickly and we proceeded to load up the hoist bucket with dirt.

Big Joe pulled the cord and the bucket took off like a rocket, dumping the dirt in two seconds flat. It came thundering back like an exploding grenade, shaking the foundations and everything else in the mine, including us.

I thought the bucket was going to explode into a million pieces on impact. Needless to say, my poor heart was pounding madly away and I kept well clear of Big Joe's souped-up hoist.

He was a would-be Mr Fixit who was always fiddling with his equipment. The only trouble was that, once he messed everything up no one could figure out how to get it back to working normally. His hoist was living proof of his genius; it had a mind of its own and it scared the hell out of me.

Most hoists work at a nice leisurely pace with no undue noise or speed to frighten the living daylights out of anyone. If the bucket had exploded on impact we would not have survived, and I was amazed it hadn't, considering the speed it was travelling. Maybe I should have notified NASA; they could sure have used someone like Big Joe to soup up their rockets.

I thanked Big Joe for his kindness, made my excuses and started the long climb back up the ladder. My legs were now jelly and my breathing laboured; any second I thought I was going to join the mosquitoes as I finally gasped my way out of the mine shaft.

I wobbled over to my camp and nearly collapsed when I glimpsed myself in the mirror. I was covered in fine black soot from head to toe and I looked like something out of the 'Black and White Minstrel Show'. With horror, I thought of the fumes I had been inhaling. So I politely declined Big Joe's further offers to teach me how to mine. I decided to stick to my mine and hopefully survive this outback adventure. But if I hadn't sold my house in the city, I think I would have packed my bags and headed back to the comforts of civilisation there and then.

I was still having no luck in trying to find a suitable hoist. A day or two later the Professor offered me the use of his short-throw hoist and truck until I could purchase my own hoist. I wanted a long-throw hoist which dumps the opal dirt away from the mine shaft so I wouldn't need to purchase a truck to cart the dirt away. Most of the miners out here use the long-throw hoists which are cheaper and much more convenient. I gratefully accepted and made ready for my big event.

A few of the miners came down the mine with me for a couple of days to show me the ropes. There I was, going flat out on my little seventeen-pound Makita jackhammer, and it was bloody hard work. I thought it was going to kill me: how did they do it?

The joke was on me and the miners all had a good laugh before showing me how to use the jackhammer correctly. They played this little prank on all the newcomers to the field. The miners made out they were a really tough bunch, as if there is nothing at all to using a jackhammer. They stood there with the jackhammer in one hand and a cigarette in the other. There was no need to break your back pushing and shoving the jackhammer through the dirt and rock; all one had to do was hold it properly and gently guide it through the dirt. It did all the work, thank the Lord.

I was now in business and loving every minute of it.

The Kangaroo Hop

Now the mine was set up and operational, it was time to buy a field car. My poor little nine-year-old Gemini sedan was doing it tough; I'd already lost the whole muffler system and both shock absorbers. My car was falling to bits from the rough tracks and corrugations in the non-existent roads. Screws were falling out everywhere from the shaking and I really didn't know what was holding the car together.

I managed to purchase an old Toyota utility for $100. I think it was about thirty years old or more and I'd never seen a car like it. One of my neighbours managed to get it going for me and he drove it to my camp with my Gemini's battery in it.

I needed another battery and a spare jerry can. I had never thought about the difference in petrol; the generator uses standard and cars use super. I thought I would have to find opal soon with all these extra expenses I hadn't counted on.

I also had to learn how to drive the Toyota, which had gears. After years in an automatic, this was a major effort. The Professor gave me a quick rundown on the gears and left me and Sunshine, his wife, who didn't drive, to our own devices.

We thought we would go out collecting some wood for my open fire. After spraying the car for the redback spiders that were crawling everywhere, we substituted pillows for the non-existent seat cushions to protect ourselves from the springs and climbed aboard.

After the initial shock of takeoff and the kangaroo hops all around the field, the old bomb went like a charm. I soon puttered around in first gear, as the grinding and crunching noise of the gears every time I tried to change them brought howls of laughter from everyone. Besides, I thought low gear was safer: the ute had no brakes.

Learning Experiences

A couple of miners set the generator up in the back of the ute for me, which was great. I could now drive over to the mine, drive back to camp and use the generator, so I now had some electricity of my own. I set myself up all cosy ready to start my generator and have a night of lights and music, but I couldn't get the generator to start. Big Joe came over and gave me a hand, telling me the generator wasn't getting enough air. The air filter was dirty, so I had to wash it out the next day and wait for it to dry before I could use it again.

I was also having second thoughts about setting up the generator in the back of the ute as I had no room now to collect wood for my fire and nowhere to put the dogs when Sunshine accompanied me on my trips around the field. I also didn't like the generator jumping all over the place on rough tracks. I really needed a shed to be built in a hurry so I could set the generator up properly, then just run a lead from it to the camp and the mine.

I readied myself for the night ahead, confident the generator would be fine now that I had cleaned the filter. It started straight away and I settled myself down for at least four hours of electricity.

I was sewing some curtains for the camp, my music was blaring away and my hundred-watt light bulb was shining beautifully when everything conked out. A fierce wind was blowing and I went outside with my torch to see what the problem was. I had left two plastic garbage bags next to the generator, and the wind had blown them onto it, blocking off air access to the filter and melting all over the generator. I was amazed at my stupidity, and it served me right for not thinking. I went to bed muttering and cursing, hoping the garbage bags, intended to protect it from the rain, hadn't damaged my newly bought generator. I was obviously going to learn things the hard way; I'd just have to get a shed built.

Big Joe checked the generator over for me the next day; thank God there was no damage. He offered to sell me twenty-five sheets of iron at five dollars a sheet so I could build my shed and I gratefully accepted. They really were a nice bunch of people out there, and so very helpful to all newcomers, which made life a lot easier.

The Professor converted my radio-cassette to run off my car battery so I could listen to music without having to worry about setting up the generator. It was too expensive to run just for lights and music anyway, so I decided to use it only for mining purposes and the occasional night for lights.

The Deluge

The rain clouds were building up again, with everyone predicting a mini-flood. Thank goodness I had the opal dirt built up all around my camp.

I had to disconnect my radio-cassette from the car battery in case of rain, so I was back to silence again. I didn't know whether I would have been better off buying ordinary batteries; at least I would have had some music to listen to. I hoped to be fully organised soon; all these little problems because of the weather!

The rain started pouring down one night at 1.30 am. I was drenched as I raced outside to close my window flaps and make sure the generator was fully covered. I had forgotten about the mine being open but it was pitch black and the rain and the wind were horrific.

Blow it, I thought; the mine would just have to take its chances. After all, it would dry out eventually, I hoped. It certainly didn't pay to be unprepared for anything out there.

By morning I had a raging creek at the back of my camp, though fortunately the water was diverted by Big Joe's opal-dirt wall. I would have been flooded out otherwise.

It rained for three solid days without a break. It was awful. All roads into town were out, as were virtually all tracks on the field. Everyone was on foot. The mail couldn't get through. No mining could be done for weeks until the holes were dry and pumped free of water. I was desperate for a nice hot shower.

All my wood got wet, everything was damp and mouldy. My dirt floor and carpet were spongy to walk on and I was trapped in an unbelievable environment. To think I gave up civilisation for this: no, I'm not a closet masochist, I like my comforts.

The sun finally came out and put me in a better frame of mind. I managed to get a fire going and heat some water for a shower. After hearing me moaning about everything, Drongo Charlie offered to sell me an old wood stove. I could set it up inside my camp, so I wouldn't have to worry about the weather and my open fire any more. I was delighted and paid him to set it up for me. We just cut a hole in the wall for the small chimney to fit through as it was only a very small wood stove. I could sit there and feed kindling-wood into it.

I was ecstatic until I lit the stupid thing and it smoked me out of the camp. It just had too many cracks and holes in it and I moved it outside, next to the open fire. At least I could still use it when the wind whipped up, not worrying .about burning my camp down with the open fire. It was so dry out there that an open fire was too dangerous when it was windy.

The Big Con

Now I had settled in, the miners pounced on me to work the bar at our little social club. As bar duties were voluntary and the club was a non-profit one, I would be paid the princely sum of five dollars a night, for a shift starting at four in the afternoon and lasting until the last person left the premises, anything from ten until three or four in the morning.

They even tried to talk me into doing the cooking on Friday and Saturday nights; the club put a meal on if the members could find someone silly enough to prepare it. They had an old wood stove out the back and that was it. All rather primitive.

They were a very persuasive lot, but I drew the line at cooking, offering to work only two nights a week to help out. I also drew the line at volunteering to chop wood for the fire.

I thought working in the club would be a good opportunity to get to know everybody, and perhaps to pick up some tips on mining; the main topic of conversation was who was getting opal and who wasn't.

What they very conveniently neglected to tell me was that I also had to clean the club, fill the kero fridges and freezers, cart in the firewood, get the fire going, cart out all the rubbish and start the big thumper of a generator. I had been conned all right, but I accepted with my usual sense of good humour. No wonder they couldn't get anyone to run the bar.

Being a non-drinker, I was a real asset. I didn't guzzle all the profits away like so many before me had. I was now accepted as a bona fide miner as well. Now I was really enjoying most aspects of my new lifestyle.

A TOUCH OF TRAUMA

Robyn McWilliam

We are all a statistic in some way or other, but for me, facing the greatest killer of women in Australia — one in eleven — came as an unexpected challenge.

From the time one nipple swelled days before the other when I was twelve, I grew to like my breasts. Many women were dissatisfied, thinking theirs too small or too large. But my bosoms balanced my body. By sixteen I had a 36–24–36 figure, the 1960s ideal in inches.

My breasts were like beacons; merely touching them through a jumper sent boyfriends into a frenzy. I was more interested in kissing, then skipping into the house before boys became more demanding. Throughout those virginal adolescent years I could not see my breasts' sexual relevance. The only time I envied girls with smaller breasts was when I yearned to wear skimpy tank tops without the necessity for a bra. I had to be in lacy underwired bras and was far too modest to reveal a curvaceous cleavage. I walked with my chest stuck out, confident and proud of the firmness of those breasts.

Marriage, then babies in my twenties, wrought ruination. Discovering I had unattractive feeding bags came as a shock: expansion then veins like blue rivers running across my breasts were all part of their biological destiny. After the birth of a son, my milk factories were huge and overproductive. I ended up at Tresillian with feeding problems, was introduced to the breast pump and developed some sympathy for dairy cows. My stock of milk was frozen to help feed other babies. While I fought to get my figure back, my breasts drooped sadly on my chest. A few years later, when my daughter was born, they dropped even further.

Through my thirties fluid retention caused breast pain before a period. Increasing vitamin B intake or taking the new drugs for premenstrual tension were the answer; it was all quite normal, my gynaecologist assured me. But one year after Christmas my breasts were so sore that I thought something must be wrong. They swelled up and touching them was agony for a couple of days until my period began the deflating process. I now feel this was a sign of breast disease.

Friends talked of breast cancer, speculating that one of us might succumb. I never seriously considered it; I knew I was in the low-risk bracket because I'd had children and breastfed them. My breast self-examinations were cursory. They felt lumpy all over to me: how could I detect a pea-sized lump that might give trouble? I relied on an annual checkup.

In September 1986 my right breast blew up to the size of a football. I wasn't premenstrual either; this was hardly normal. Luckily I went to my GP. He believed the cause was a cyst and referred me to a surgeon to have it syringed.

The specialist's room was dark and dingy with its timber panelling. He was old and full of self-importance in his white coat. First came questions, then examination. The swelling had gone down but the specialist discovered a large lump that he estimated at five centimetres by two-and-a-half. Unable to find his tape, he went looking for a ruler with which to measure my round lump. As a former science teacher, I was unimpressed.

I tried to ascertain what was wrong with my body but

the specialist seemed reluctant to give me any information. When he talked of surgery, I said I wanted a second opinion. Inflating himself like a puffer fish, he said, 'Do you realise who I am?'

'No,' I said. 'I don't know if you're any good or not.'

Then came his final patronising remark: 'You little ladies read too many horror stories in the *Women's Weekly*.'

He obviously had no idea he was talking to a career woman who read literary fiction. Tears of frustration came as a reaction and I walked out.

They say you get the medical treatment you deserve: fortunately I wasn't the yes-doctor type, and followed my intuition. Since then, it has been established that the more assertive you are in seeking the right medical treatment, the better your chances of survival. There was no way I was going to let that doddering old fool I saw first put a scalpel to my body.

Then began the search to find a surgeon I might have faith in. A first cousin whom I hadn't contacted in years told me of the surgeon who had done her mastectomy. I was only facing a lumpectomy but I had not realised there was a family history of cancer. My mother had died of bowel cancer at fifty-two but I had separated the types in my mind, even forgetting that she'd had a benign breast lump removed in her final months. My faith in doctors had been sorely shaken at the time: she had been the oncology department's guinea-pig for some tests and mistakes were made in her treatment.

When I walked into the bright modern room of my new surgeon, I made it clear I knew enough about the body to understand explanations. Some people don't want to know what's wrong inside but I felt that if he couldn't communicate, I wouldn't trust him to operate. This time the vibes were right. I'd have to have tests, but the lump would still have to come out.

I had my first mammogram. My breasts were

squashed into extraordinary shapes to picture their internal structure. The report showed no cancer, nothing to worry about. Then came the ultrasound where a sensor over my cream-covered breast showed sections of its interior on a TV screen. The lump area was assessed as hormonal fluid. I went back to the surgeon with two negative tests but the lump still had to be removed. We made a date: 19 November.

I love the way doctors talk of 'popping you into hospital' for a few days. First you must survive Admissions where you're left unsure of your own identity by the time endless forms are filled out. Then comes the blood test. I drew Clinic 13 reaffirming my superstition that this wasn't going to be pleasant. The man before me was reprimanded because he had not followed procedure. I sat beside the table of phials, needles: implements of blood letting. The nurse's face had hardly recovered from her scowl but I could see from her sharp lips that she was not the chatty type.

Businesslike, she placed my arm in front of her. The black tourniquet tightened as I hoped my vein would be responsive. I didn't wish to parade bruises at the weekend. Skin puncturing has medieval connotations for me; leeches to remove foul humours. Two phials were filled and I wondered what tests my fluid would be subjected to: AIDS? Maybe they would find something else; a worry when one is feeling fine. I went to the ward with my belongings stuffed in a red Australian Pacific tour bag. Pity it wasn't a holiday. More questions: the resident doctor was a young woman. Only my mother's death from cancer made her pen hesitate.

Next morning the blood retriever returned. Hormone tests. Her face was still as sharp as her needles. Then I was off to theatre garbed in elastic stockings and white gown. The trolley ride: corridors from the horizontal position. I was petrified. My face was turned to one side so any

escaping tear of self-pity soaked into the pillow. My surgeon was present, he squeezed my hand. My lump was
probably benign he said, ninety-five per cent are.

I awoke that evening. Beyond the grey-filmed glass the
weather was wild, gales of wind, slurries of rain. Was it an
omen? My surgeon looked worried; he was talking of
black nodules around the lump he removed. It was 20
November. Six long days to wait for the pathology report.

I'll never forget that phone call. My mother-in-law was
helping me chop the fruit for the Christmas pudding, from
an old recipe I used every year for our boisterous crowd.
The surgeon's voice. He read the report. All I detected was
the word 'carcinoma' and I went numb. He didn't even say
'cancer' but after my mother it meant one thing to me — a
death sentence. How could this be happening to me?
Married, two children, hardly a sick day in my life. I had a
feeling I mightn't make it to old age. But at thirty-eight I
felt far too young.

Tears and fear engulfed me and I headed to the comfort
of my bed. A girlfriend rang. She drove over, we cried in
each other's arms. Later my husband, son and daughter
came home. More tears. I couldn't bear the thought of not
seeing my children grow to adulthood. How would their
father cope when they turned to me for so much? The
worst afternoon of my life dragged on. I didn't get up
again. Exhausted, I finally fell asleep.

The surgeon suggested my husband and I come and see
him together. We were into December when getting away
after Christmas was uppermost in everyone's minds. His
opinion: only radical mastectomy would save my life.
He'd seen inside my breast, described black nodules
around two or three other precancerous sites. He wanted
to remove the offending structure straight away. Two years
later we would talk about reconstruction; especially as I
was a younger woman. *He's waiting to see if I die or not,* I
thought. Wasn't this about being positive? I knew I was a

coward when it came to operations. Give me time away from hospitals and I wouldn't come back for cosmetic reasons. The psychological damage of being horribly lopsided haunted me.

'Tell me all the options,' I heard myself say. He mentioned immediate reconstruction, a plastic surgeon's name.

'I don't think we could schedule surgery time together before Christmas — we shouldn't wait,' he said. I left with a referral.

The plastic surgeon was a quiet man with a gentle touch. He outlined two choices, did the pinch test on my abdomen and said I didn't have enough flesh there to create a boob the size of my other one. He'd put in a tissue expander to stretch my own skin. It meant a valve under the skin, saline injections every week and a final operation to put in the silicon implant. As far as was known in 1986, they were quite safe; silicon was inert in the human body. Lots of women had been enhancing their breast size with implants. When I'd made my decision, miraculously they found the surgery time.

Going into hospital again on 10 December was more scary: my first major surgery. They were going to hack off half my chest. At least I'd averted waking up totally lopsided. The following day was lost from my life. After premed I went into theatre at ten in the morning, woke to see my husband's face about 7:30 pm before drifting away again.

Next morning I was quite chirpy, exploring the various connections to my body. My chest had corset-like packing from which emerged three tubes leading to bottles under the bed. I thought the nurse called them 'red-i-backs' and wondered how spiders came into it. The later pronunciation of 'redivacs' made it clear they were for drainage, collecting red ooze from my body. The drip taped into the back of my hand became an object of hate by the next day. I looked at the contraption of suspended plastic bags and tubes, hoping it would keep operating. Nurses came in and flicked it as if goading it into behaving. Large doses of antibiotics were fed into me to stop rejection of the implant. By afternoon I was delighted to have the drip removed.

Helplessness made me frightened. I couldn't even sit up by myself. Days earlier I had walked into the hospital; now I was too weak to move my body. I had been clenching my fist and trying to move my right arm as the doctor had told me. Regaining movement in it was a major priority. I had to work through the pain. I hated being a useless right-hander.

In the late afternoon I was helped out of bed to sit in a chair. I put on headphones and went into a world beyond hospital bustle. The soothing effect on my body made me believe in music therapy. I felt so much better, a tiny speck of enjoyment seeping back into my life. My mind and body were too traumatised for me to concentrate on reading but taking in sound intensified healing.

Finally the dressing came off. Clips and puckering skin stretched for ten centimetres. 'Yuk' was my mental reaction. The plastic surgeon gave me a local anaesthetic and injected saline into the tissue expander. It felt strange to have the needle clicking into the hidden valve, then a tightening in my newly swelling breast. The staff must have admired my control as they asked me to talk to a woman who had screamed at her scar. She never came to see me. I wonder how she would cope in the future. On leaving hospital I was given a record of my stay. I read my post-operative recovery was excellent.

One final agony was taking out the last redivac. Nearly thirty centimetres of tubing had been in my chest ten days, cells clinging to its surface, and removing it was like wrenching out part of my body. Deep breathing and fingernails cutting into my palms were my only aids. Afterwards I was sweat-soaked and weak, wanting only to crawl under the covers.

How happy I was to be let out on Saturday. I wanted to see my friends so we went to a dinner dance. Dressing up was great after hospital gowns. With make-up and a little extra padding in my bra I looked normal from the outside, not like a woman who'd undergone a mastectomy. But I felt pitifully weak within. We tried one dance but I was paranoid about being bumped. Fragility was a new experience. I would have to learn patience during my long recovery.

Once home, I realised the wonderful support I had had from extended family, friends and business associates. I had missed the Christmas parties but was not forgotten. My hospital room had every species of bloom a florist had to offer; wall-to-wall colour. Visiting hours rarely went by without a smiling face to brighten me up. The experience taught me to value friends and family highly and always visit others in hospital.

When I was three days out of hospital we moved house, our first move in seventeen years. Before I knew of the lumpectomy we had bought a new home at auction and sold the old one a week later. All the real estate dealings had escaped me as doctors became the centre of my life. The removalists had to do most of the work; I was a barely mobile supervisor. A neighbour and a girlfriend made the beds and put away the kitchen goods in the new house. I was so grateful and eventually found most things. My bed looked out a bay window to a huge liquidambar tree. Seeing its luxuriant green growth was somehow reassuring. I hoped to see many seasons of its leaves changing to rust and falling, then a verdant coating reappearing in spring.

Weekly injections of saline began. My skin stretched, as it had in pregnancy, but this time to accommodate the implant. Throughout January school holidays children ran all over the new house. How I craved quiet to rest. Not forgetting to exercise my arm every day to avoid threatened physiotherapy, I began swimming across the shallow end of the pool, fearful of sinking for the first time since childhood.

Twice, too much fluid in the expander brought nights of excruciating pain and I felt the skin on my chest would pop open. Back to hospital. The ache, despite medication, had me pacing the house, tears flooding over my cheeks. Surely my new breast would be worth it. My plastic surgeon told me others had given up, which made me more determined to tough it out.

In May 1987 I went back to the dreaded smell of floor wax and antiseptic. The routine of getting to my hospital bed was easier for the third time round in six months. The tissue expander would be replaced by the implant. I awoke from surgery with an oxygen mask on. Breathing was difficult due to the packing completely encircling me; I felt like an American gridiron player with slipped padding. I had another temperamental drip; checked thirty-five times during the night. Victory: it was removed next morning. Then I had to undergo more blood letting. No arm veins were suitable so the ambulance trainee gouged it from my ankle. Now the mere mention of blood tests brings images of passing out.

My new breast was disappointing but at least the implant was soft, a satisfactory bulge so that in a bra the mutilation and subsequent patching would be difficult to detect. A day of depression was followed by a blacker night. How I yearned for dinners, wine and dancing. Would I have these again in my life? Somehow my old optimism seeped through. The saying 'life begins at forty' lightened the sense of hovering doom. I must make it to the promised age and not think of a recurrence.

No use yearning for my former breast; it had been a killer. My ability to cope with anything distressing was zero at that moment, but I knew I'd get stronger day by day. The treatment was finished; I had been reassembled. A life of husband, children and my writing awaited me.

And I had already learnt that tranquillity, good nutrition, positive thinking and the will to live are vital ingredients needed for recovery. I hadn't been through all this just to turn my face to the wall and die.

The plastic surgeon wanted one more operation, to fashion a nipple. I can't blame him for wanting to finish the job but his talk of skin grafts determined my stance to remain nippleless. I'd had enough of hospitals. Pain, appointments and tests had monopolised my life for too long. I was lucky to have found my cancer early and avoided follow-up treatment of radiotherapy or chemotherapy because my lymph glands were clear. Cancer cells had not begun their move to other parts of my body.

Since my treatment I have learned so much about breast cancer. Books, seminars, clippings from the newspapers; it seems there's been an explosion of material. The first thing I did after it was all over was go to a stress management class, having filled out a questionnaire about stress while I was in hospital. Two years earlier I had been superwoman, with a full-time job, house, husband and children to look after. Every day my head spinning with the effort of organisation, all my responsibility. It had brought me close to burnout and I'd resigned from teaching.

Before my experience, I hadn't seen myself as a particularly stressed person; nor had others. A sense of humour had always helped me appreciate the wacky side of life. But when I began to yell when woken early on a Saturday, I knew I had to quit. I liked earning good money but I felt trapped. All I wanted to do was rest.

The first time I entered the relaxation state I felt so great I didn't want to come out of it. A mesmerising voice, a state of calm, my mind in a kind of wishy-washy euphoria. I adjusted my priorities; so many daily trivialities are just not worth getting into a state about. Sometime later I was ten minutes late for a committee meeting.

'You're late, we couldn't start,' one woman exploded.
'Everything's fine. I'm here now. It's not exactly Hiroshima,' I said, thinking, *This woman is damaging herself, getting so uptight.* As part of stress therapy I was introduced to soothing pipe music. New Age music, blending peaceful nature sounds and certain instruments, has abounded since.

Yoga and meditation gave me a far greater awareness of my body and the power of the mind. These are now touted as the tools to handle our fast-track lives. Once you regain control you can opt to slow down. Busyness is a disease. I felt I hadn't watched the grass grow since I was a child; perhaps that is why I looked back nostalgically on that time. Our trainer told us to learn to please ourselves, put things into our days that we enjoyed, sweep guilt feelings from our minds and expunge the word *'should'* from our vocabularies.

If the magical shape or colour of a crystal enticed me, I bought it. I learned to indulge myself. The aroma of oils, sounds of nature, feel of crystals and seeing mystical paintings were part of a renewed appeal to the senses. They seemed to convey the message that each day is precious.

I could have been dead before forty and I was determined to enjoy every single day, to be more open to absorbing life's pleasures. The feel of water swishing around my body when swimming, the deep purple of a pansy, taking time to listen to a friend. And I've come across many who'll pressure you into their way, trying to dump guilt on you. To a few heavies I've mentioned the dreaded 'C' to instantly end an argument.

Self-esteem I've had to work on. So often mastectomy is associated with mutilation. The first article of clothing I bought after hospital was a tiny chemise to wear in bed and shield the difference in my breasts. During lovemaking, the scar was a concern. A few weeks later my husband asked why I wore it and now, discarded, it remains in my lingerie drawer. He was glad to have me alive and did not see me as disfigured. Reading in a magazine that one man said he was 'sick of making love to damaged goods' really angered me. How many women have loved men returning mutilated after war? Who knows how any one of us may be left after a car accident? If love is extinguished by a scar, it was barely an ember.

Clothes buying became irritating: no more underwired bras as something soft around the implant was required and a slight lopsided effect had to be camouflaged. This was even worse with swimming costumes. The string bikinis of my early thirties were gone forever; tight-fitting tops or dresses never seemed to look right. I adopted loose and elegant as my fashion statement.

Two behavioural reactions stayed with me. I get extremely upset when I hear of breast cancer sufferers who didn't make it. The actor Jill Ireland was so motivated to help others by her experience that I saved every clipping about her. Then she died. I had to watch several women I had met die of the disease. One who had talked to me before my operation had been so positive: her death affected me for weeks. The experience makes you reassess if you're doing enough to save yourself. Will the cancer return if I don't meditate or eat the right foods?

In about September each year, I had a period of feeling unwell and immediately suspected a recurrence: was this the beginning of my end? Someone told me the body cells were remembering their trauma. But I feel any pain that persists for more than a week must have a sinister origin. My disease robbed me of feeling secure about my health, though I haven't suffered painful fluid retention in my left breast since the diseased one was removed. My confidence improved after the five-year all-clear checkup. Annual visits for life were still on the agenda. I, who thought myself invincible, have been forced to face my own mortality.

It was also important for me to work out in my mind why I got the disease. My family is vulnerable to cancer: my mother died early, my father has since had prostate cancer. There is a link between this and their daughter's breast cancer, though the stress of my trying to do too much was certainly a factor.

In 1994, the 'BRCA1 gene' responsible for breast cancer was isolated. Soon tests will be available for those in the high-risk bracket to be screened. One of those will no doubt be my daughter. Her breasts are a cause for worry because of my disease. It concerns me that the price of a career and family may be a woman's health.

The old high-dose contraceptive pill has recently come out as a factor after being suspected for years. At a seminar I asked whether other women had high oestrogen levels, indicated by bad morning sickness. Hands went up around the room; eighty per cent had that symptom. For all of us hormone replacement therapy for difficult menopause is out of the question: too much oestrogen is a major factor in breast cancer. But now new drugs are being developed to fight it.

But it has been shown that cutting fat, protein and alcohol intake, eating certain vegetables and avoiding obesity all cut down chances of further trouble. Nurturing the immune system is vital; not letting anxiety and stress unbalance it, increasing susceptibility to disease. I have become quite protective of mine.

Some problems I have to live with. I had some swelling and pain in my arm for the first year or so. On odd nights discomfort stopped me sleeping on the implant side. My new breast is colder to touch than the other one, but at least it's covered by my skin. Women who don't have reconstruction have their problems. One told me she'd bought a prosthesis to fill the empty side of her bra. She was on the dance floor when her partner began touching that side and nothing made him desist. Putting her hand down her front, she said, 'If you like it so much, take it.' She left him on the floor, falsie in hand.

Five years after my treatment, the panic over silicon implants hit: damage to tissue if they leak, immune system diseases. I went back to my plastic surgeon who assured me my type had no leakage problems. He gave me a folder of warnings he was now required to give to patients. Silicon implants were banned in New South Wales in 1993. Compensation cases are raging in America. Some women here raced to have them out and replaced with saline ones. Reluctant to enter any hospital unless it's a life or death matter, I still feel I've a time bomb strapped under my chest.

Are women aware? We've had major media coverage of breast cancer. It's killing more than 2,500 Australian women each year. Incidence rose twenty-five per cent from 1975 to 1991. While there are free mammograms for women over forty they may not be the magic answer. I remember the concern on my surgeon's face; each year his patients were younger and younger. Women outside cities are disadvantaged. Two years ago it was estimated that more than half of breast cancer sufferers are receiving second-rate treatment.

I have come to regard breasts differently. Kate Llewellyn's poem 'Breasts'[1] ends with a timely reminder.

> But like life they are not glamorous
>   merely dangerous

To understand their life cycle we must give those projections on our chest far greater consideration. Breasts. How much they signify for a woman. There's a saying: Love your disease. I can't say my affection for breast cancer was great, but what happened did compel me to explore the subject. At my lowest ebb I cried at night, desperately wanting to go back to before it happened. I wanted my old breast in its familiar place, but then I would have had to relinquish life itself.

I now earn less money working part-time as a tutor and writing the GAN (Great Australian Novel). Making time for voracious reading allows the discovery of many stimulating books. Each week I go sailing on Pittwater. Some days it's a white-capped exhilarating ride, others a drifting in lighter breezes. My bushwalking group provides companionship and a greater recognition of wildflowers in our area, from fluffy flannel flowers to brilliant red waratahs, all part of our morning's escape from suburbia. And my family appreciate a more contented me.

Sure I was lucky. I've had breast cancer and survived. What stays with me is how powerfully I have been taught to cherish every day.

---

[1] 'Breasts' by Kate Llewellyn, courtesy of Curtis Brown (Aust) Pty Ltd.

MEMORY

Rae Luckie

It was years before we realised there was something really wrong with Nana. Of course looking back there was a pattern, but you don't see it at the time. I guess the penny dropped when Barry and I drove to Parkes to see her over the October long weekend in 1988. Donna, who lived around the corner and kept an eye on her had phoned and said she'd been acting strangely. We knocked at the door but Nana didn't answer. Barry opened the door calling out, 'Mum, are you there?'

She was sitting in front of the television, watching black specks on a snowy background and listening to the static. It was nearly lunchtime, the weather was quite warm and she was wearing a faded blue velour dressing gown, slippers, mittens and a striped hand-knitted beanie. Framed photos of her grandkids smiled down from the walls and there was a thin sprinkle of dust on the plastic flowers blooming in green pots in the slatted wooden stand. A pile of assorted photograph albums was stacked on the coffee table and she had one open in her lap.

We gave her a kiss, she smiled, Barry fixed up the television and then offered to make us a cup of tea. 'Meals on Wheels will be here in a minute,' she said. Barry picked up the electric jug and beckoned me over; the element was covered with sliced peaches. 'How about you get dressed and we'll go the Leagues Club for lunch,' I said.

'Oh, no,' Nana said. 'Meals on Wheels will be here in a minute.'

'Barry, do the children have far to go to school?' She was sipping her hot black tea with one saccharin tablet and gazing at a school photo of our three kids.
I started to explain that now they were twenty-six, twenty-three and twenty-two. 'Don't you remember Shane called in on the way through to Dubbo a few weeks ago?' I said.

She gave a funny little laugh, 'Oh yes, sometimes my brain does silly things. Meals on Wheels will be here in a minute.' In the beginning I thought it was the usual kind of forgetting associated with getting old. After all, she was nearly eighty.

Donna arrived a few minutes later. I laughed and said 'Meals on Wheels must be pretty good. Nana would rather that than go to the club.'

'There's no Meals on Wheels at weekends,' Donna replied. We wandered outside. Donna worked as a home help for the Community Services Department but Nana was a friend, not a 'client' as they like to say.

'She can't be left alone much longer. She keeps on hiding things and losing things. She forgets everything. I go around three times a day, the nurses come to bathe her but she's starting to do dangerous things. Yesterday she tidied up and stacked all the newspapers on the hot plates.'

We had made enquiries at Rosedurnate nursing home a couple of months earlier, but Barry's sister Gayle wouldn't hear of it. 'Mum is okay. There's nothing wrong with her,' she said. Gayle lived in Brisbane with her husband and three kids and Nana used to stay there for the school holidays, looking after them and helping out in their newsagency.

A year or two earlier Nana had stopped writing to us. At the time I thought she just didn't care about us any more because she seemed totally wrapped in Gayle and her family. I used to write regularly and signed everything: 'Tons of love, Rae and Barry'. Then, 'Tons of love, Rae Barry & Trish'; then, 'Tons of love, Rae Barry Trish and Tracy'. Then 'Tons of love, Rae Barry Trish Tracy and Shane'.

Now it's 'Tons of love, Rae and Barry' again, and there's no Nana to write to. She was cremated in Brisbane. A month later Gayle brought her ashes back to Parkes. We assembled from Sydney and Parkes and Broken Hill and Brisbane and stood at Pop's grave which had been discreetly opened while the little cask and worn gold wedding band were placed inside:

Here lies Mary Boyd McNaught Luckie
a loving wife mother and grandmother.
Rest in Peace with Doug.

We had asked Nana what she wanted to do. 'I want to stay in Parkes. I don't want to be a burden on anyone,' she said. Gayle decided to take her to Brisbane to live. That was the beginning of the great confusion. Nana would never again piece together the new patterns of her life.

Barry went back to help Nana pack. He made three trips to the Parkes rubbish tip, her memories travelling along Brolgan Road and dumped. She gave Barry four scrapbooks, riddled with silverfish tracks with some of the pages yellowing with age. One had been kept during the war and three had all the letters our kids had written. I had always

been a letter writer and made
the kids do the same. There were
four and five letters layered on
top of each other on every page
with clippings from newspapers
and old school reports.

Dear Nana and Pop
I love you. I am 6.
That is the sky.

Tracy and Tricia used to
draw stick figures dressed in
square trousers and triangle
skirts and houses and suns and
stars and flowers and trees. Shane used to draw buses,
trucks, planes, helicopters and steam trains, all with flash-
ing blue lights. Just like on Dad's grey Holden police car.

They drew with crayons
then coloured pencils then
water paints and textas and
pictures made out of
coloured pieces of kindergarten squares ripped and
stuck down with Clag from
the office. Sometimes they
included the date stamp
from daddy's desk.

7 May 1968

Dear Nana and pop and gayle and snoopy daddy had a
loan of a new mini police car and then he crashed. love
from Tracy

He would have been killed, but the safety belt saved
him. So he got safety belts fitted in our old blue Wolseley
straight away. When Pop died we used to take Nana on

holidays to the caravan park at Bermagui or Laurieton so we had another one put in. It was the only car I knew with four safety belts in the back. Tracy hated seat belts and talked herself into getting car sick as soon as she was restrained. Click clack front and back. She'd always try to sneak it undone. Had to watch her all the time. Watch as she'd get paler and paler and look for somewhere to pull off the road where she could be sick.

Dear nanna and poppy and gayle
I have got the mumps. And my face is all swollen up. thankyou for the letter and the ribbon. I liked them very much. I have some pink pills. The school was going on an Excursion. But I cannot go. Tracy is home from hospitle. I have to stop home for two weeks. I love you all. from Tricia

Dear Nanna and Pop
How are you? Yesterday I went to Burrendong Dam with Alison. When we got there Alison and I went for a swim. After a while we got some grease on our hands. Alison said rub sand on them so I did. So then I got some sloppy mud and I said why don't we make a mud bath and we did and we rolled in it. love from your most trublesum grandchild Tracy

Funny how the letters plot our lives. Now we mostly talk on the phone and there's nothing to go back to. I mean, you don't really remember a phone conversation years and years later, and you can't pick it up and hold it and sit and remember. I keep promising myself I'll write to my kids, but you know how it is when there's no time left to do what really matters.

Dear Nanna

Hope you are well. Hope you can come down and visit us some day. cause we all miss you. Today at hockey our team won with is called Bega primary 2. My teacheres name is Mr Partriadge, he is the sports master. When I came he said to me "Would you like to play hockey because they were making a third team and needed one more player to make up there team. Our team one a medal each it was gold. At Kiama we stopped at the blow hole and watched it blow. It is really good and if you go up the stairs and along the path you can see where the water starts to go in. The cat and dog had to stay in the old police station witch is beeing built up. Our house is really nice and I love my room.

Love
Tracy

Dear nanna and pop.
I think i left my key at your place. When i am nine i am going to get a bike. I keep on loseing my voice. matty comes up nearly every day. And he has swims in our big pool. And he allso rides his two wheeler up and he lets me ride it a bit. Around the little road. He might be coming up again on Satureday. tons of love

Nana kept the letters Pop wrote during the war.

29/3/1940
Dear Mary and Barry
   So far I am still O.K., but sweating like a pig, one of these days I be just a grease spot. I am receiving your letters regularly now so I can always expect them on each Tuesday or Wednesday and am always able to sit down for a quiet half hours read of it. I always read it two or three times to make sure I haven't missed anything. I especially enjoy reading about Barry's sayings and doings. He is starting to talk very well now, no doubt they are great mimics aren't they, he must be just getting interesting.
   We might be going into *****CENSORED***** next Saturday on leave. Hope we get paid before we go in. I have money to collect but at present only have 30 cents which is about 1/-. Now I can start and answer your letters. There is no need to worry about the censors, so far they haven't even opened your mail, all ours is censored but so long as we do not mention certain things our letters go through alright.
   Don't forget to let me know about Barry anytime he is sick. I always want to know about him, what he says and what he does, I really think I am missing out on the best time with him, never mind the war will be over by 1942, so it won't be long before we get together again.
   Have to have a shave before I turn in, think I had better make it a quick one or I'll have the officers coming after me.
   By the time you get this you will be in your new home. Hope everything is as you like it and Barry doesn't knock the place about too much. He would be quite excited about seeing his Grandma again.
   Give my love to all you folk and a big kiss and a hug for Barry. I'd love to see him even if it was only for half an hour.

Love from Doug.   J.M. HORDERN (CENSOR)

She kept her letters the Army sent back ... unopened.

26/12/41
77 Amherst Street North Sydney

Hello dear,
Well how did you spend Christmas Day, not too good I suppose, did you hang up your stocking, or doesn't Santi go that far afield. The best present I received was a letter from you which came on Christmas Eve. I was feeling a bit down in the dumps hoping I'd get one before the holidays and it did arrive...Christmas Eve I went over to H Park to help them at the shop and we were very rushed. Dode was down and Tony and oh my she's fat and Doug she was so cranky and hardly spoke all day. It appears Tony has been cranky (teething) and she's so quick tempered with him, anyway I kept out of her road which is the best way, we would have had an enjoyable time if something dreadful hadn't happened.
Uncle ordered 24 dressed fowls and had 20 odd of them ordered by women and the fowls didn't turn up, oh my, if things weren't hot, so by 8 o'clock, after we held off a dozen women and you can imagine what they would be like and I can quite understand them being like that as they were stranded. Uncle sent the girl help up to the junction and she managed to get four dressed ones and uncle got four live ones and they had to start at 9 o'clock and kill clean and dress 4 chooks. I caught my stocking on a tin box and ripped it to pieces and stockings are like gold now ....
When I got home Mum had got Barry off to sleep and he had hung up his stocking, bless his heart, so I had to proceed to fill it, I wanted you badly dear ....

and after nine more closely written fading ink-pen pages...

Well dearest I'll have to leave you until next Sunday so until then my dear look after yourself for Barry and I we need you. Just try and write whenever you can, I'll understand.
Lots of love till next week from your loving wife,
Mary
Barry's latest is 'mine daddies in 'Laya' tilling Germans'.

30/1/42

*...Twelve months to-morrow
dear, isn't it a long time, let's
hope and pray they send
some help to you and everything goes well from now on.*

*Don't ever forget that
Barry and I think of you
every minute of every day
dear and long for your safe
return. So until I write
again on Sunday night I'll
say cheerio*

    from your loving wife

              Mary

8/2/42

    *...how worried I am about
you dear. I do hope you
are well and safe it's some
weeks now since I heard
from you....*

**ARMY POSTAL SERVICES
DELIVERY IMPRACTICABLE
RETURN TO SENDER**

13/7/42

Dear Madam
    With reference to my recent letter inform-
ing you of the absence of news concerning
your Husband Number NX 50912 Corporal Douglas
Gordon Luckie 8th Division Provost Company
A.I.F.
    I am directed by the Minister for the Army
to advise you that he must now be posted as
Missing, and to again convey to you the
Minister's sincere sympathy. Your natural
anxiety at the non receipt of further partic-
ulars is appreciated and you are assured that
everything possible is being done by the
Department...

She never gave up hope. She
put ads in the *Sydney Morning
Herald:*

SINGAPORE:
Any information of Cpl.
Douglas Luckie, 8th Div.
Provost Coy., would be gladly
apprec. Please comm. Mrs
D.G. Luckie, 77 Amherst
Street, North Sydney.

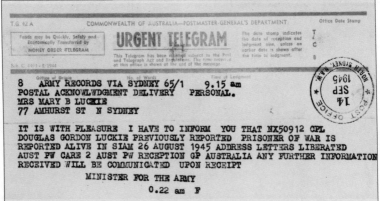

He'd been in Changi and on the Burma Railway. One of
the lucky ones to survive.

1976
Dear Nanna
Little athletics has started again and I'm going to it. At gymnastics Kendy Hobs has taught us a dance that we have to do at Police Citicins Boys Club. for the kids there. Also were doing a dance for the widdows wich I think you know about. We've missed dad and hope you look after him. Shane and me watched the ABBA specil wile Jenny and tricia went to the pictures to see JAWS.
Love Tracy

Suppose you want to know why the kids were missing, Barry? And did you notice it was 'Dear Nana' instead of 'Dear Nana and Pop?'

We had been transferred to Mudgee a couple of years earlier. It was great living so close to Nana and Pop. Pop and his old mate Ronnie Jones were helping his next-door neighbour Bob who was ill. They offered to do his Sunday morning paper run to Bogan Gate. Bob's son was to show them where to go and what to do.

PARKES CHAMPION POST
FEB 11, 1976

Condition 'Unchanged'

Douglas Luckie (70), a pensioner, of the Military Road Parkes, received a suspected broken neck in a car accident near Bogan Gate on Sunday Feb 8 last.

He was flown to Sydney by Air Ambulance on Sunday afternoon in a serious condition.

On arrival at Kingsford Smith Airport, he was placed into an ambulance and transported to Royal North Shore Hospital.

Police escorted the ambulance which had to travel at under eight kilometres an hour from Mascot to the hospital.

Doctors feared the slightest bump or jolt could have put his life in danger.

A spokesman for the hospital said yesterday that Mr Luckie's condition was 'unchanged'.

Mr Luckie was a passenger in a car which was travelling east along the Parkes–Condobolin Road and left the road and overturned several times.

The vehicle was extensively damaged and the driver and another passenger were both injured.

The driver, Greg Parsons (17), suffered bruising and shock, and the passenger Ronald Jones (66) suffered a fractured collarbone and extensive lacerations and bruising.

Both were admitted to Parkes District Hospital.

A spokesman for the hospital said yesterday that Jones' condition was 'improving'.

The spokesman pointed out that Parsons was due for discharge yesterday.

At first I didn't worry when the Police truck arrived at home that Sunday morning. But then they asked for Barry to go outside and I saw him go white and then he came inside and grabbed a few clothes.

Ronnie's nephew, 'Little Ronnie' — who is married to Donna — arranged to meet him at Orange with Nana. And so began the vigil at Royal North Shore with Dr Yeo in attendance.

Four days later Barry rang and said I'd better come as they thought Pop was going to die.

Johnno drove me to Sydney. The kids called him 'Mr J'. He and Barry escorted Tricia to her first school social in sixth class. I'd made her a long jade blue skirt and a pretty top. 'You look so beautiful,' he said to her, 'that I am going to marry you when you grow up.' She laughed. Later she used to baby-sit his son.

Johnno was a Vietnam vet who joined the police force when he came home. He and Barry (the Sarge) were friends. Mr J had a wife and a little boy. She tried to have another but she kept miscarrying. He kept getting red raw rashes and he would rip his clothes off and scratch and get under the shower, even at work. They tried to find out what the matter was and he would get depressed. One day his wife left him.

Barry got a phone call in the middle of the night. When he went over, Johnno was sitting with his .38 Smith and Wesson and a Hornet rifle beside him. Johnno said he was going to kill himself. Barry sat with him all night while they talked and Johnno drank. Two bottles of whisky and one of Karloff Vodka through the long night and into the day. Johnno said he owed Barry his life and they transferred him away because his wife had left him. Then he met someone else and they had two little girls and they were happy.

We used to call in to see them at Toronto on the way to Hawks Nest for holidays. One day he was sitting with his two little girls on his lap, looked at his wife and smiled at us and said, 'You know, I owe this guy everything,' and he hugged the kids. Then he got stomach cancer and died.

All the way to Royal North Shore, where Pop was, I ranted and raved and Johnno listened. When we got to the hospital Barry was waiting in the car park. They shook hands and he said, 'Thanks, mate.' Then I realised that Barry looked ten years older.

We sat in the waiting room at Royal North Shore and went in two by two. Keep your head down as you walk in. Don't look at the other seven beds full of pain and suffering. Just head for Pop.

His skull was drilled on both sides to hold the screws for traction. He was quadriplegic with no chance of walking and he couldn't speak. Tracheostomy. Tubes everywhere. His eyes pleaded and tears dripped. We took turns at wiping them away and sat and crooned and told him not to worry and we loved him and rubbed his forehead. Then we had to go outside and cried some more and waited.

Thirty-three days in intensive care.

The waiting room was in a corner of casualty so we were drawn into everyone else's tragedies. The mother of an athletic sixteen-year-old who'd fallen out of a tree at Yanco. She sat in the waiting room and cried because he said, 'Don't worry, Mum, I can learn to type with my mouth.' She wiped her eyes, put on a lipstick smile and went in to her son again.

Nana never gave up hope.

I went home to Mudgee and collected the kids from various friends' houses. Barry stayed.

Three months later, sixth floor, Royal North Shore. Pop could finally talk. He used to plead with Barry and me to kill him. To end it. Never in front of Nana or Gayle.

'Please help me end it,' he'd beg. And you helped to feed
him and scratch his head. Sometimes he thought he was
back on the Burma Railway. He'd refuse to eat. Share it
with the others or there'll be a riot. The lice are driving
me mad.

There was nothing they could do. But technology
breathed for him and kept him alive.

Thinner and weaker.

He died after seven months.

Nana lived alone in Parkes for the next thirteen years.
Of course we'd visit and she'd go to Brisbane for holidays
and call in and see us on the way back. But the letters
stopped.

We phoned Nana every Sunday in Brisbane. It's easy to
blame your mother-in-law's daughter but I still think the
move from Parkes was the beginning of Nana's total confusion. She didn't seem to know where she was and kept
telling Barry and me that she wanted to go back to Parkes. I
wrote to Gayle and told her Nana seemed so unhappy. I
suggested maybe she could go back to Rosedurnate in
Parkes where most of her old friends were living out their
days.

```
    Dear Barry and Rae                    2/1/91

    Well, thankyou for your card and lovely let-
ter which I received Christmas eve after work.
I have sort of been expecting it but really
amazed at the same time.  I was so furious that
I sat down and read it to Mum and asked her if
this is where she wanted to be or did she wish
to go to Rosedurnate.
    She didn't really know what was going on but
I think she is more cunning than we think
because the next phone call she sounded a lot
happier over the phone.  I know that she really
seemed to miss you — but hate to say it, but
```

never says she misses you or wants you or even
talks of you unless I bring it up... She
thought that you lived just near us I think
until we explained to her and made her realise
that you lived a long way away ...
    Dr Johnson says she needs to go on a diet and
lose weight but that is hopeless as when I am
not home she eats all the biscuits, lollies,
anything that is about. She eats ice cream and
then puts it in the fridge, uses the butter and
puts it in the freezer, uses the orange juice
and spills (& leaves it) on the floor — eats
frozen fish fingers ... Mum weighs 95 kgs and
it affects her walking as it is very difficult
carrying so much weight ... I truly am sorry
that I haven't written but you too are at fault
— so don't blame me entirely. As you can imagine with a family of 5 plus mum and working
full time I don't get much time for myself ...
The kids just grow up too quickly these days.
Your kids too, I wish we had all written more
often and swapped photos too.
    Well, too late now.
    Bye for now, lots love Gayle XXX

Nana came to stay at Springwood in October 1992, so
Gayle could have a break. I wasn't sure I could cope. I'd
never seen Nana without her clothes on. Folds of flabby
skin and warts and huge black moles in abundance. She
wasn't embarrassed; guess she had got used to the people
Gayle had coming in to bathe her. 'You shouldn't have to
do this, Rae,' was all she said. But at the finish we made
it a game. Trusting and helpless. False teeth in the
Steradent. But first scrub and scrape and gouge off a year
of growth.
    Reminded me of when the kids were little. Just talked
my way through. Adjust the water. Hold her hands as she
manages to unsteadily step into the shower recess. Is that

okay? Towel on the recess floor to stop her slipping. Now, try not to touch the taps. Hang on to me instead. Now I'm just going to wash your back ... and now your bottom ... and now your legs. Every day I get soaked through as well. We laugh together.

We organised a party for her eighty-fourth birthday. She hadn't seen her older sister Peg, and cousin Bunts for over a year. Circulate dips and nibbles around ancient legs and a walking frame. Iced sponge with jam and cream. Blow out the candles in the shape of eighty-four. Sing happy birthday. Sip wine in best crystal. Presents. Red paper serviettes. Munch on honey chicken wings, rice salad and Black Forest cake.

We get out the old photo albums and I look at Nana and Auntie Peg and Bunts and think  how I hate the thought of getting old and losing my mind and having other people make my decisions. The party is over.

We sit on the verandah — her and I. Watch the wind in the gum trees and the red and green king parrots and red and blue rosellas that come to the seed tray. 'Just like on the Arnott's biscuit tin,' she smiles.

Memories start to surface. Tells me her Dad was a

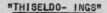

> "THISELDO- INGS"
>
> NO. 25.
>
> MISS. MARY McNAUGHT.
>
> "HERE'S MARY McNAUGHT,
> THE LATEST WE'VE CAUGHT,
> IN THISELDO'S BIG TENNIS NET,
> AND TAKE IT FROM ME,
> AS YOU WILL SOON SEE,
> SHE'S THE BEST WE'VE LANDED AS YET".
>
> WITH HILDA, FOR YEARS,
> PALS HAVE BEEN - THE DEARS -
> AND NOW THEY'RE TOGETHER AGAIN,
> THEY'RE BOTH IN ONE TEAM,
> O.K. IT DID SEEM,
> AND THAT THEY WILL WIN SEEMS QUITE PLAIN.
>
> NOT LONG DID IT TAKE,
> HER NAME HERE TO MAKE,
> MIXED DOUBLES SOON CAME TO HER LOT,
> TO FINISH THIS RHYME -
> WHEN SHE STARTS TO CLIMB,
> THE LADDER, SOME WILL GET IT HOT.

plumber on Garden Island and she lived in Balmain when she was a girl. She played tennis. 'I couldn't afford to go to White City,' she said and she'd laugh and sigh and gaze at the blue sky laced through the gum leaves and say it reminds her of Parkes.

'I think there's something wrong with my brain,' she said.

'What happened to Doug?' she asks.

And we talk about their house and the garden and the kids and the war and the accident. I feel guilty when she goes back to Brisbane but we phone her each Sunday.

Nana's memory worsened and she couldn't be left home alone, so Gayle put her in the Neilsen nursing home for sufferers of dementia. We began to dread the Sunday phone calls because Nana would often cry. 'Why am I here. Why am I in jail? '

Helpless; guilty.

One more trip to Springwood for Christmas 1992. She meets her six-month-old great-grand-daughter from Broken Hill. Still confused but gentle, kind and placid. 'Placid' was her nickname on Betty Muczyczuk's radio  station 2PK Sunshine Club. They raised millions of dollars for the Far West Children's Home in Manly.

She learned to sit and wait and hope.

'What happened to Doug?' she asks.

One day she cried. 'Nana, what's the matter?' She looked up at me.

'Why can't things just stay the same?'

And so on a perfect April day in 1994 we gathered in the Parkes Presbyterian Church.

I didn't mourn the shell that had died, but wept for the woman who faithfully waited for her beloved to come home from the war.

KIT

Rae Luckie

April 1991: It's strange sitting with the childless Kit —
almost as if she's the embodiment of the three dead sisters.
Each of us three 'nieces', Jan, Rae and Pat, children of
Madge, Nell and Anne, see our mothers represented in her.
Having lived with Madge and Anne I can see all three. We
sit and talk and wait.

Most aunts and mothers I guess you'd kiss and hug.
Not the four Chandler sisters. I often wonder why. Kit was
the youngest and she and my mother Nell were close in
age and temperament. Headstrong. Kit loved friends, fun,
and hockey and dancing — merrily going her own way,
living up to her jolly, happy, fat girl life-of-the-party image.
She wasn't interested in the family newsagency in Peisley
Street Orange before or after her mother died.

OBITUARY
December 30, 1938

Though it was known to her many friends and relatives
that her health had been of an indifferent nature for some
time, necessitating a visit to Sydney for special treatment,
the announcement of the death of Mrs Madge Chandler,
of Peisley Street, which occurred at St George District
Hospital, Sydney, on Wednesday last, will be received
with the deepest regret by many residents throughout the
town and district of Orange.

Mrs Chandler, who was 57 years of age, was a
native of Orange, being a daughter of the late Mr and
Mrs John Livingstone, members of the old pioneering

family, prominently identified in the early days with German's Hill, now Lidster, on the Cargo Road, and who, in the latter stages of their well-spent life, conducted a small store on the corner of Summer and Sale Streets, where Mr H. Swain subsequently built a butcher's shop.

It was there Miss Madge Livingstone spent her girlhood days and grew to womanhood in the midst of many life-long school friends, who always admired her for her fine characteristics and loving devotedness to her aged parents. Later she married Mr Harry Chandler, a highly-esteemed and capable agent, of Peisley Street, and, following his death fourteen years ago, Mrs Chandler, with her young family, remained in the same premises, until her death, and, ably assisted by two daughters, conducted a successful newsagency and stationery business.

Mrs Chandler was always a valuable citizen, and, always imbued with a great deal of enthusiasm and a progressive spirit, rendered inestimable services to a number of public and charitable institutions. Her work, perhaps, was better known in connection with the Orange High School Parents' and Citizens' Association, with which she had been actively associated for several years, and held the position of Hon. Secretary with conspicuous success from 1919 to 1925, the methodical manner which the books were kept and monthly meetings recorded being often freely commented upon. Her valued services were highly eulogised by the late headmaster, Mr A. M. Armstrong, and other members, when a presentation was made to her on the occasion of her relinquishing the secretarial duties. Her interest in the affairs of the O.H.S. was further pronounced when she presented a medal, known as the Chandler Medal, for the dux of the school. Mrs Chandler's untiring efforts for many years were also directed towards the old District Hospital and the Presbyterian Church, both bodies benefiting because of her interest and benevolence. The deepest sympathy will be extended to the members of her family in their irreparable loss, Madge (Mrs Blandford, Orange), Ann (Mrs Bleechmore, Parkes), Charles (Sydney), Nell and Kit (Orange). There are five grandchildren. The funeral will leave her late residence, 139 Peisley Street, at 11 a.m. for the Presbyterian portion of the Orange cemetery.

Some friends of Kit's had started their nursing training in Canberra shortly afterwards and had resigned *en masse* after being unable to work for the disciplinarian Matron Guy. The matron at Parkes district hospital took them on and allowed two years of their previous training. Kit thought she might try nursing with them at Parkes. She lasted a month.

Kit gives a little sigh as the sister comes in with the purple slow-release morphine tablet in a tiny pleated white throw-away paper cup. 'You know I used to get away with blue murder, being the youngest. Madge had to do everything for Nell and me. She cooked for us and sewed for us and looked after us when Mum went away. Dad spoiled Nell and me until he died. When I started nursing at Parkes I just couldn't take the discipline. No one was going to boss me around and tell me what to do, so I went back home to Orange.'

Bowls for major ops.
Boil 30 mins.
6 large bowls
1 medium bowl
3 smaller bowls
9 small lotion bowls
4 lge. kidney trays
3 flat trays
1 instrument stand tray
1 two-pint measure
2 wash-up room bowls
3 nail brushes

Kit decided to have her second try at nursing in 1940 when Nell married Ken Kelly and he moved into the Chandler family home and business. Kit had a row with Ken, moved out and began training at Forbes.

Sister smiles cheerily as she hands Kit a tiny pleated paper cup. 'Here's your Maxillon tablet, dear, it will help stop the nausea.' Kit painfully swallows. I pick up her worn beige handbag with the packet of Turf and yellow lighter inside and we walk out to the balcony. Smoke drifts up.

She chuckled, thinking back to Forbes hospital. 'I was always ready for a dare — Macker dared me to ride my bike through the male ward. I did, madly ringing the bell in the middle of the night. I don't know how I didn't get the sack. There was a ward attendant (I forget his name now) — we used to give him curry. One night we put Macker on a slab in the mortuary covered with a sheet. When he walked in she slowly rose up.' Kit pauses and chuckles, 'He ran out screaming and, honestly, we never saw him again.'

Two more Turfs ('You must hate this smoke going over you.' 'No, I don't mind,' I say) and we go back to the ward. She takes a couple of sips of pumpkin soup, but can't be tempted with anything else. Trays full of food going back to the kitchen. The sister smiles and comes in with a tablet in a tiny little white pleated paper cup.

Tonsillectomy and Curettage of Adenoids
1 tonsil guillotine
1 mouth gag
1 tonsil snare
1 tongue depressor
1 scissors
1 sucker and tubing
1 pillar retractors
1 blunt adenoid curette
1 scalpel for dissection
1 sharp adenoid curette
6 curved Howard Kellys forceps
1 tonsil forceps
6 straight Howard Kellys forceps
Gut for ligatures

Sometimes I spent the school holidays with Nell in Sydney, and once she took me to visit Kit, who was living in the nurses' home at Wollongong hospital. I loved the winding, clattering ride on the train from Sydney to Wollongong, glimpses of the sparkling sea through rainforest. Kit and Nell sat on the narrow bed and drank beer and talked and talked and ate fresh white bread and butter and tinned asparagus. I was bored and couldn't understand their pleasure as they dug wet sloppy stalks straight from the tin. Kit was a big full-busted no-nonsense woman with a wacky sense of humour, large smiling nicotine-stained teeth and fingers never far from her favourite red packet of Turf cigarettes. Nell was the opposite, totally slim and trim, but like Kit she always had a cigarette in the rusty-coloured fingers.

Kit entertained me singing 'Three Little Fishes' in a put-on falsetto lispy babyish voice:

Down in a meada in a liddle widdy pool
Fwam free widdle fishies an a mumma fishie too
Fwim said the mumma fishie Fwim if you can
An they swam an they swam all over the dam.

Boop boop diddam daddum wantum choo
Boop boop diddam daddum wantum choo
Boop boop diddam daddum wantum choo
What the old folks say is always true.

The dietitian tries to tempt her. 'You must try and eat something to keep your strength up. Would you like to try some asparagus?'

So frail helping her up — a hug for a woman you never hugged. Thin bloated arms cling around your neck. Pat the back, feel the shoulder blades — sharp and bony, sticking out. 'Let's go on the balcony.' So she can have a cigarette or two, or three. It's getting too cold to go there now. Adjust the body in the chair to ease the pain. Sit and talk for a while. 'Can I go inside now?'

'No I don't want any surgical interference,' she said.
Mostly it's the indignity that she hates.
'I just can't stand it any more. I can bear pain but I just
can't stand this any more.'
But she has no choice.
I kiss her goodbye. 'I hope you have a good night's
sleep.' Her anguished eyes meet mine. 'I just want to go to
sleep and never wake again.' But she does wake. Bad days.
Worse days.

Kit and Arthur met late in life. Kit was almost forty
when they got together. They came to visit Madge in
Orange, to get her oldest sister's 'seal of approval'. Sunday
morning. I'm riding down the hill to get the Sunday
papers. My plaits flying in the wind down the Peisley
Street hill. Wheeeee!! I pedal as fast as I can — take my feet
off the pedals and they go round and round and round I
try to get my feet back on — too late — out of control in
the loose gravel at the bottom of the hill.

I wheel my battered bike back up the hill bawling
loudly. Blood trickling down my leg from a deep wide
gash below the right knee. Bits of gravel under the skin.
'Now stop snivelling over a little thing like that,' says Kit
matter-of-factly. 'You should see what it's like in the operating theatre at Camden — this is absolutely nothing.' So
she washes and cleans and bandages. I stop crying. Can't
be a sook, have to be brave. I've still got the boomerang-
shaped scar.

I was very suspicious about her and Arthur, billing and
cooing and holding hands. Giving each other butterfly
kisses. I didn't approve as I expected grown-ups not to
behave in such a manner. Affection was not for public dis-
play, or private for that matter.

Kit 'n' Arthur settled happily into a government-built
duplex near Civic in Canberra. They had a dog, Simon
called Peter. Also known as Pete and Fud or Fuddy. He'd
sit beside the table, a piece of Kraft Cheddar placed on his

nose. Waiting for the signal to eat it. Good boy, Fuddy. They'd show off his range of tricks, 'Look Fuddy, there's a fly. Catch the fly.' Simon called Pete would yowl, growl, leap and snap and catch the unsuspecting fly. Wag and pat.

'Come on, Fuddy, talk, there's a good boy.' He'd whine and seemingly have a conversation. Wag and pat. 'Play dead, Fuddy, beg Fuddy, roll over Fuddy, clap your paws, yes, yes,' they'd croon, 'he's a good little boy.' Wag wag wag. Pat and scratch and pat. Their little baby, but he wasn't allowed to sleep indoors. Bedtime. Come on, get your rug, Fuddy. He'd pick up his rug in his strong teeth and fall in behind Arthur, stretching his neck for a scratch and a pat.

They gardened. Probably the best vegie patch in Canberra. Kept all their neighbours supplied. When you visited you went home with tomatoes and beetroot, marrows and cucumbers and pumpkin and capsicum (how about some carrots and parsnips too?). A few fruit trees carefully grafted, pruned and trimmed, guarded from the dreaded fruit fly. Visit late summer and you took home deep purple Satsuma plums and Kit's recipe for plum sauce.

> *6 lb plums*
>
> *3 lb sugar*
>
> *3 pints good malt vinegar*
>
> *2 level teaspoons salt*
> *$1/2$ level teaspoon cayenne pepper*
>
> *1 level teaspoon allspice*
>
> *1 level teaspoon cloves*
> *$1/2$ cup green (crushed) or dry ginger*
>
> *Boil all slowly for two hours.*
>
> *Rub through a sieve.*
>
> *When cold, bottle, cork and seal with paraffin wax.*

Kit always said she couldn't cook.

Poetry as She is Wrote

The brook is rippling
Rippling is the brook
The cook is snivelling,
Snivelling is the cook
The idiot that started this
Should have her gullet on a hook.
(As per fish).

KSC

She cleaned through the house every day and made her beds with hospital corners.

They brewed their own beer. 'There's no such thing as a bad beer,' Kit would say. 'There's good beer and better beer.'

Arthur would come home from work. They'd talk baby talk to each other, just like they did to Fuddy. It used to make me cringe. He'd give her a peck on the cheek. Kit would smile. 'Here's your slippers, love.' Weekday tea grilled chops and three veg prepared ready to go on top of the stove. She'd settle Arthur down and bring in two bottles of beer. They'd sit together, resting on gaily coloured hand-crocheted cushions and Arthur would fill Kit in on his day at Commonwealth Motors where he was foreman.

After tea they played canasta and listened to ABC radio. Kit 'n' Arthur loved fishing 'down the coast' but had no time for those who took away all the mod cons or stayed in on-site vans. For them, fishing and camping meant roughing it. They would load up their Holden station wagon with a mattress Kit made to fit, chuck in a primus, a frying pan and the rods. They always caught a feed. Arthur cast his own sinkers and carefully bound his rods with rows and rows of coloured thread. One he made from cane had a champagne cork for a stopper at the end of the handle. Kit gave it to my husband, Barry, when

Arthur died. We take it to Hawks Nest every year. I always think about Kit and Arthur at Hawks Nest.

Arthur died of lung cancer fourteen years before Kit. I wasn't surprised. You used to hear him and Kit coughing in concert late at night and early morning in the cool Canberra chill when you stayed with them. She nursed him at home until the last. He wanted to die at home. Nell went down to stay with her. It was October 1977. Nell rang me.

'Guess what?' she says.

'What?' I say.

'Arthur is being cremated and Kit and I are sitting here at home having a couple of quiet beers, remembering.'

I don't know what to say. Silence. 'Oh,' I say. Nell tries to explain.

'Well, Kit and Arthur agreed there'd be no false hand-wringing after he went. Anyone who wanted to say good-bye had, and that is that.'

'Oh,' I say.

'And I want you to do the same for me when I go or I'll come back and haunt you. No funeral, no hand-wringing, no nothing. I don't want you or anyone there. Kit and I have made a pact to do the same.'

Nell died two weeks later.

Poetry or Not?

When I quit this mortal sphere,
To mosey 'round, I won't be near,
Don't weep or cry, laugh or sob;
When my feet are burning on hell's hob.

Don't go and fling a large bouquet,
Upon my chest, it doesn't pay;
Don't mope around and feel all blue —
I'll be better off than you.

> *Don't kid yourself I was a saint*
> *Don't smear my name with pure white paint;*
> *If you have 'jam' like that to spread*
> *Tell the world, before I'm dead.*
>
> *Say it with flowers and curse my soul*
> *I'd like one rose within my buttonhole*
> *My wishes, like friends are very few*
> *But what are friends when I've had you?'*
>
> *KSC*

Kit was alone the last fourteen years. She still gardened and kept in touch with her sisters' children. Letters written in copperplate. The centre of the tenuous net linking the relatives. Filled each of us in on the other's doings and sometimes gave advice. 'Of course I'm good at bringing up other people's children,' the childless Kit would say.

We were holidaying at Hawks Nest when we got the phone message that Kit had cancer. My cousin Jan called from Canberra. 'Kit has a large tumour on the lung. Could be a couple of weeks or a couple of months.' I go across and sit on the beach. Death and holidays seem to go together. I want to think about Kit and gather my thoughts before I phone her. The Gulf War intrudes when two FA18s from Williamtown roar along the waterline.

'I'm just so tired,' Kit said when I rang. 'But I want to get everything in order. I suppose it's self-inflicted. I don't want to leave anything for others to worry about — but I seem to be a bit aimless. I washed a whole lot of things, you know, bras I hadn't worn for years and then put them back in the drawers. I've paid for my cremation. I don't want anyone there.'

'No, I won't have any surgical interference,' she said.

The next weekend we drove to Canberra. Kit had

cleaned up her house and burnt most of her past. She was worried about the weeds overtaking the garden. Green garbage bags ready for St Vinnie's. 'Is there anything you would like?'

'No,' I say. She gives me a marcasite mouse my mother gave her forty years before and some doilies she crocheted herself. A Stewart crystal vase: 'I want you to have it. They gave it to me when I left Camden hospital.' A Chinese good luck ornament my mother's friend, Mary Pang, had given her, some photos of her mum and dad and Nell, some obituaries and a little silver bookmark with a butterfly on it. 'I want you to have them,' she said.

This do in remembrance of me.

Dirge No 1

> This universe is dull,
> And love's a fetter,
> No happiness can gull this world so dull,
> Where life is little better;
> So take this parting gift from me,
> A cigarette, book and alcohol,
> Now I will make my own damned hell,
> Where none can pity, my poor lost soul.
>
> KSC

She started talking about the past.

'Dad died when I was seven. He was a great scholar, and so many people were illiterate that much of his living was earned writing for others.' Kit had thin carbon copies of some of the letters. She showed me her favourite in her father's perfect copperplate:

'Devella Springs'
Via Kerrs Creek
10th March 1903

Miss Isabella Travena
C/o Mrs Dubois
Restaurant
Summer Street
Orange

Dear Isabella

I am very much distressed by reason of your uncalled for refusal to carry out your promise to marry me.

As you know, I have intensely loved you for more than eight months past and I was quite willing to overlook the past and will be gladly content to do so in the future if you carry out your promise and marry me.

I have done all that a man could do to meet your wishes.

Do like a good dear girl think well over the matter and favour me with a reply as early as possible.

I am heartbroken.

Yours faithfully,

Thomas John Goodwin

HC

'I wonder what happened to Isabella,' said Kit. She handed me a white album with some yellowing paper cuttings inside.

OBITUARY
Mr Harry Chandler
April 22, 1926

There was widespread and genuine sorrow in Orange and district yesterday when it became known that Mr Harry Chandler, of Peisley Street, had passed away suddenly. For some time, Mr Chandler had not enjoyed robust health. Firstly, heart trouble manifested itself, and then he suffered a slight stroke, but care and home attention appeared to have worked a desirable improvement, and he led a fairly active life until a few hours before the end came, with startling suddenness. On Wednesday he accompanied his wife to the Show, but, as the afternoon advanced, he complained of feeling unwell, and they returned home. Doctors were called at once, and the services of a nurse obtained, and at about 11 o'clock, he rallied sufficiently to peruse a newspaper. Shortly before 6 o'clock yesterday morning, he asked for a stimulant, and, whilst this was being obtained for him, he passed away ...

Kit gave a little sigh as the sister came in with the purple slow-release morphine tablet in a tiny pleated white throw-away paper cup.

'We all used to get new dresses for the Orange show. It was the big occasion of the year. Mum and Dad used to cook ham and corned beef in the copper to help with the meals served in the luncheon tent. There weren't many cars and the train trip was part of the excitement of going to the show. We didn't get a car until after Dad died. Mum learnt to drive. She got an Essex and then a Buick. In between she had a Ford coupe and she'd sit in the front with Anne. Nell and I would sit in the dickie seat. She crashed it and Anne ended up in a barbed-wire fence. So Mum got rid of the Ford. I think Madge resented Mum. Mum used to love theatre and so when Dame Nellie Melba or Anna Pavlova or Paderewski went to Sydney Dad would arrange with our half-brother Les Chandler to get tickets. He would put her on the train to be collected by Les and Nell and I were left with Madge who had to look after us. Mum went down to six stone before she died — it was cancer too.'

Another walk so she could have a smoke on the balcony.

'I'm scared,' she said.

Pat and her husband come to stay. At Kit's. We drive back to Springwood. And back again. Each weekend. Six of us on the balcony. With Kit.

Waiting.

Kit shrinking. Eyes glazed and milky looking, pupils dilated. Her thin face plumped with fluid. Her hands weep, streaming rivulets. Fluid-filled face washers strung up, drying out. But she can't sit still. Not even for a minute. 'I've got to get up,' she said. 'I've got to keep moving.' She painfully gets to her feet.

'Can I help you?' I ask.

'No I'm all right,' she said.

She walks two paces unsteadily, hands on hips. It was the last time she got out on the balcony. Stares out at the golden day. Over the hills eucalypts on one side, the other suburbia, but a suburbia where crimson claret ash and yellow maple hide the regulation red roofs. 'Canberra is so beautiful in the autumn,' I tell her. 'It is so dry between here and Sydney but the trees are beautiful.'

I describe the autumn brilliance driving through Mittagong, and the road near Lake George. You turn a corner, the lake is sparkling on the left — on the right-hand curve a magnificent stand of every autumn tree imaginable. Each trip I rave about it until the leaves start to brown and fall.

Her hands are no longer swollen, because the skin has broken down and weeping streams of body fluid continually trickle out of the cracked skin. Kit is bluish-looking, needing oxygen. 'I'm away with the fairies again,' she says, 'I know it's the morphine, I can feel the jolt at different times.' Maxillon for the nausea, Duphalac for the bowels — the body becomes obsessed with the pain of the bowel, the burning rectum, the ruptured anus. The indignity of pads to catch the uncontrollable, enemas and bleeding haemorrhoids. 'At least the bleeding eases the pressure,' she says. For a while.

No food, nothing to excrete. Just pain and suffering.

Kit has finished looking, walks to the right, turns around and sits painfully down. Moaning. 'I can't take it

any more. The burning pain in the rectum and around the
anus,' she says. Clinical talk, a flash of the old Sister
Chandler. 'They gave me another enema — it's knocked
me around.' She doesn't eat. Sips of water, a little soup,
and every now and again after the exertion of going to the
toilet a few whiffs of oxygen.

Pat and I stand waiting for the lift to Ward 5E. 'Just
thought I'd warn you. Kit is a bit upset today. Someone
stole her handbag last night. They found it on the second
floor. Forty dollars was taken. It wasn't the money that
upset her. The thought of someone creeping next to her
bed in the middle of the night. Robbing a dying woman.'

Bastard.

We go back to Kit's with Pat. 'You might like this photo
I found of your mother.' I was looking for a little silver
bookmark. I gave it to Kit. I'd like to have it back. I stay
silent. Guilty. Remembering the promise to Kit. 'I want
you to have it,' she said.

She's still trying to organise her life after death. 'Don't
forget to write to the girls when I'm gone,' she reminds
Jan. 'The names are marked in the address book near the
phone.' The 'girls' are nurses she had trained with all those
years ago.

I saw Kit on the Sunday, three days before she died. She
weeps. 'I must have been so bad, so bad.'

'What do you mean?' I ask.

'I must have been so bad to be punished like this,' she
says.

The pain. Too weak to walk. Too weak to talk. Morphine
drip, double the dose. 'Thanks for coming,' she whispers as
I pat her head and hold her hand. So tiny and wrinkled and
shrivelled. She reminds me of the wise monkey. 'I love
you,' I whisper.

'I love you too,' she says.

As I walk out I remember another of her ditties.

I went to the elephants' fair
All the birds and the beasts were there
By the light of the moon the giddy baboon
Was combing his auburn hair
The monkey he got drunk
He fell on the elephant's trunk
The elephant sneezed
And fell on his knees
And that's the end of the monk the monk
And that's the end of the monk.

Kitty Stewart Chandler died on 8 May 1991. No notice, no funeral, no obituary, no flowers, no sorrow, no friends, no chance to grieve, no nothing allowed. But I find a few pieces of paper in a box that belonged to her sister, Madge. Some lists of surgical instruments to learn by rote. Some poetry signed many years ago with a copperplate KSC.

RJP

Beneath this silent stone is laid
A noisy, Antiquated maid,
So please pass on, don't idly waste your time,
On bad biography or bitter rhyme,
What I am, this cumbrous clay ensures.
And what I was, is no affair of yours!

KSC